Diary of a Cricket Season

Diary
of a
Cricket Season

Bob Willis

Pelham Books
London

First printed in Great Britain by
PELHAM BOOKS LTD
52 Bedford Square
London WC1B 3EF
1979

*Photographs by
Patrick Eagar and Ken Kelly*

ISBN 0 7207 1084 7

Photoset, printed and bound
in Great Britain by
REDWOOD BURN LTD,
Trowbridge & Esher

Contents

Illustrations

13. Graham Gooch in action during his innings of 94 for England v. New Zealand, Prudential Trophy match (*Ken Kelly*)

Between pages 96 and 97

14. Mark Burgess lbw to Willis, first Test v. New Zealand, 1978 (*Patrick Eagar*)
15. Delight from the England team as Geoff Howarth is out at the Oval (*Patrick Eagar*)
16. Burgess gets well beneath another Willis bouncer at the Oval (*Patrick Eagar*)
17. A boundary off Steve Boock gives David Gower his maiden Test century at the Oval (*Ken Kelly*)
18. David Smith in the process of making his 132 not out for Warwickshire v. Sussex (*Ken Kelly*)
19. Two fast bowlers in action during the 1978 season: Richard Hadlee and Bob Willis (*Ken Kelly*)
20. Geoff Boycott wipes the sweat from his brow after scoring a century for England v. New Zealand at Trent Bridge (*Ken Kelly*)
21. Mike Brearley during his 50 in the Trent Bridge Test (*Ken Kelly*)
22. New Zealand opening batsman Bob Anderson is run out at Trent Bridge (*Ken Kelly*)
23. Bob Willis batting during the third Test v. New Zealand (*Patrick Eagar*)
24. Umpire Dickie Bird checks Willis for overstepping at Lord's (*Patrick Eagar*)

Acknowledgement

The author is grateful to Alan Lee for his help in compiling this book

Introduction

On the day that the 1978 cricket season ended, I managed at once to feel satisfaction, gratitude, regret, depression – and overwhelming fatigue. For the previous twenty-six months, I had played cricket almost without a break, which for a fast bowler is a punishing sentence in itself. But there was more to it than that. The year of 1978 had promised to be eventful and, even up to September, it had exceeded expectations. It was an often confusing whirlpool, in which politics, big business and countless personalities were all caught up in a web once reserved for the actual playing of the game.

The intrusion of Kerry Packer and World Series Cricket had initiated the change, way back in May 1977. Issues were to be clouded for a considerable time to come by the influence of this man, and in 1978 I felt them as keenly as anyone, despite having resisted an admitted temptation to sign for his 'circus' in September of the previous year. My eventual decision to stay with established cricket opened vast new corridors to me, and for the first time I was able to appreciate and exploit my commercial potential as England's only genuine pace bowler.

I began the season feeling fitter and perhaps bowling faster than at any time in my career. I also began it as Warwickshire vice-captain, a post that was to bring me less pleasure than I had anticipated.

At the close of the previous season, with David Brown having made it known that he did not wish to stand again as captain, Warwickshire had appointed John Whitehouse as the man to lead them through a clear transitional phase in playing strength.

The position was not helped by the presence at Edgbaston of one Dennis Amiss, a one-time England opener now committed to Packer. There was nothing personal against Dennis, but the mere fact that he was a World Series player persuaded the rest of the playing staff that they didn't want him. The consequent wrangle, involving committee, members, players and inevitably the press, provided a disturbing backdrop to a distressing county season.

Fortunately, there was nothing distressing about England's summer. Six Tests – five wins and a washout – represented an efficient annihilation of opposition which never reached the standards we had expected. Pakistan were beaten 2–0, New Zealand whitewashed 3–0, and such easy victories inevitably diverted attention onto the personalities at the forefront.

It was always going to be a summer in which Mike Brearley continued his battle to shake off the shadow of Geoff Boycott. As soon as Mike broke his arm in Karachi in January, leaving Boycott to captain the remainder of the winter tour, that much was certain. Boycott emerged from his captaincy baptism with his reputation somewhat tarnished and Brearley was restored for the start of the summer. As he maintained his unbeaten record as Test captain, his position would have been totally secure but for the fact he hardly scored a run. It was a wretched batting season for him, and agonizing for the rest of the England players to watch. For he was the man we all wanted to lead the side to Australia and the Ashes fight.

All this, though, was very much in the future when I reported back to Edgbaston for the start of a county season that had certainly stirred me. I felt Warwickshire were on the verge of becoming a power again, and I wanted to be part of it. Little did I know how disappointed I was to feel in four months' time . . .

The Cast

The Warwickshire Playing Staff

Neal Abberley – top-order batsman, 34. Works as a travel agent and coaches at the club's indoor school. Married with two children, and a dedicated family man. Nickname 'Abbers'.

Dennis Amiss – former England opener, now playing for Kerry Packer. Despite his 35 years, I rate him as the best batsman in England apart from Boycott. His weakness against short-pitched bowling makes him a devotee of helmets. Nickname 'Sacker', for reasons unprintable.

David Brown – once England's strike bowler, still a reliable seamer at 36. Lives on a farm, where he breeds horses, racing being his next love to cricket. Chairman of the Cricketers' Association and one of my few very close friends – we try to room together at away games. Nickname 'Barnsley' after an infamous Barnsley Chop meal.

Chris Clifford – an off-spinner from Yorkshire, recommended to us by Geoff Boycott and, at 36, one of the oldest players to make a Warwickshire debut. Teaches PE. Nickname 'Wef'.

Russell Flower – spinner, played on a match basis during 1978. Nicknames 'Flower-Power' and 'Elvis', through resemblance to pop singer Elvis Costello.

Eddie Hemmings – 29-year-old off-spinner who can also make useful runs. A kind and generous fellow, happily married and now a proud Dad. Nickname 'The Whale', or 'Ernie'.

David Hopkins – young seam bowler who played occasionally during 1978, a quiet, unassuming young giant of 6ft 6in. Nickname 'Hoppy'.

Geoff Humpage – immensely talented natural batsman, and an adequate wicket-keeper who should be England's reserve if he fulfilled his potential. Married, 24 years old. Nickname 'Humpty'.

Alvin Kallicharran – fine left-handed batsman, 29 years old, new captain of the West Indies following the defection of the Packer men. A tiny man with a humour I don't often find in West Indians. Nickname 'Kalli'.

Andy Lloyd – 21-year-old Shropshire boy, very promising batsman and stop-gap bowler. Another horse-racing fan, and one of the most sociable members of the side. Nickname 'Jasper' after comedian Jasper Carrot, more for the colour of his hair than his incessant, often witty chatter.

Chris Maynard – 20-year-old deputy wicket-keeper. Fine prospect who will push to make the job his own. Nickname 'Fish'.

Phil Oliver – 22-year-old all-rounder, also from Shropshire and also very sociable. Aggressive batsman who, with his bowling improving, should become a regular member of the side. Nickname 'Ollie'.

Steve Perryman – gifted swing bowler, 22, a Brummie with a warm sense of humour and the ability to laugh at himself. Nickname 'Art', after Arthur Milton.

Steve Rouse – very strong left-arm seam bowler who sadly has suffered regularly with injuries. Married, with two children. Nickname 'Rebel'.

David Smith – improving 21-year-old opener from Newcastle, a great football fan of his home-town club and a conscientious worker at his game. Nickname 'Smithy'.

Tony Smith – 19-year-old brother of David, missed much of the season through injuries. Accident-prone, but a warm and friendly individual.

Gary Thomas – steady, obdurate batsman, locally born, captain of the county second team, champions of the Birmingham League in 1978.

John Whitehouse – captaining Warwickshire for the first time in 1978, 29 years old, a chartered accountant. Began the season as contender for the England middle order. Nickname 'Flight'.

The England Squad

Mike Brearley – 36 years old, and by the end of the 1978 season had still not lost a Test as England captain. Essentially a fair-minded man who handles players better than any captain I know. He can get edgy in his hurry to make things happen on the field, and worries a lot about his own status as a batsman. Another of my few close friends in the game. Nicknamed 'Scagg' after his fascination with Indian cultures had moved team-mate Mike Selvey to give him a long-winded title during the 1976–77 tour, Scagglethorpe being the middle part of it.

Ian Botham – has achieved so much by the age of 22 that there is no reason why he shouldn't become the greatest all-rounder in history. Overpoweringly confident and immensely talented both as a free-scoring bat and aggressive seam and swing bowler. Once knocked Ian Chappell off a bar stool and told him he would make more runs than him . . . he probably will if his current progress continues. Nickname 'Guy the Gorilla'.

Geoff Boycott – can be self-indulgent, selfish and unthinking, but can also be warm, humorous and tremendously helpful to any young player. Simply the best player in England, for all his much-discussed faults and his 37 years. A five-day player who can put pressure on others by his slow batting – but I would always back him to make most runs over a season. Nickname 'Fiery' after the speed of his batting!

Phil Edmonds – who, one month into the 1977–78 tour of Pakistan, ran the risk of joining my blacklist of players I would prefer not to socialize with. I have grown to like him by appreciating his biting humour. A man who trades sarcasm cheerfully, he is vastly improved as a left-arm spinner and, at 27, could be a long-term member of the side. Nickname 'Goat', or his middle name, Henry.

John Emburey – likeable 26-year-old off-spinner from Middlesex who joined his county partner Edmonds in the side for the last Test of the summer. Quiet and conscientious. Nickname 'Ernie', his middle name.

Graham Gooch – can be a destructive batsman. Developed rapidly into an accomplished opener during 1978. A shy and quiet 25-year-old, recently married. Nickname 'Zap', because of his Mexican-style moustache.

David Gower – has the look of a fine player in all conditions. Only 21, but a huge success in his first international season. Blond left-hander, and the archetypal sporting pin-up. Nickname 'Lulu'.

Mike Hendrick – Derbyshire seamer in his 30th year. Highly rated by the players, but has never quite fulfilled his promise as an England seamer. Witty man, married with three children. Nickname 'Hendo'.

John Lever – shares my age (29) and many of my interests and has become a very good friend. Great-hearted left-arm pace bowler, as effective anywhere overseas as in England, and the ideal, cheerful tourist. Nickname 'JK' his initials.

Geoff Miller – 26 in September of 1978 and still waiting to establish himself as an England all-rounder. A very useful bits-and-pieces player who bats capably and bowls off-spin, but is devastating at neither. A deep personality who worries a lot but has a good sense of humour and mixes well. Nickname 'Dusty'.

Chris Old – hugely talented pace bowler whose one failing is not being consistently fit enough. Another 29-year-old and a very sociable Yorkshireman, great value on a tour. Can be a match-winning performer. Nickname 'Chilly': C.Old, cold . . . chilly!

Clive Radley – a similar player to David Steele, yet more accomplished, he has made the most of a limited England chance late in his career. Socially, a reserved yet friendly character.

Married, and he and his wife spent the summer awaiting their first-born, a girl, who arrived in September. Nickname 'Grizzly' after TV character Grizzly Adams, because he often wears moccasins in the dressing room.

Graham Roope – a good county player who constantly seems to fall just short of top Test calibre as a middle-order bat. Knew him when I played at Surrey and have always got on well. Chatters endlessly. Nickname 'Cyril'.

Bob Taylor – an outstanding yet unspectacular wicketkeeper and one of the nicest men I have ever met – not a streak of malice in him. I room with him a lot on tours, and we've been close since my first MCC trip in 1970. Married with a 15-year-old son and 6-year-old daughter. Nickname 'Chat' for just that ability.

Other Characters

Tannoy – my father, who spent his life in journalism and is now retired.

Grummidge – my Canadian-born mother, who struggles to understand the game.

Bhuna – my brother David, a capable club batsman, and wicketkeeper.

Big Sue – the life-saving lass who does my laundry every week.

Cumbesy – Jim Cumbes, Worcestershire bowler and one-time professional goalkeeper. A neighbour and a fine friend.

I
Opening Spell

Whatever the realities or deficiencies afflicting its playing strength, every county will start every new season thinking that it can win something. It may take a month to disillusion it, or a week. In some cases, a day.

At Warwickshire, 1978 began in a mood of buoyancy and I was happily caught up in it. The pre-season training, under my supervision for the first time, had gone well and with a few exceptions the lads seemed reasonably fit. There was now just the matter of winning a few games.

The early weeks of the season these days are absurdly cluttered with one-day cricket. You either seem to be playing 55-over games or 40-over games; the Championship gets lost until almost the end of May. It's not an ideal system, but the sponsorship is welcome so we mustn't complain.

Saturday April 22
I'm often asked why we bother to start cricket in April, and up to now I've never been able to find an answer. Today was the perfect evidence for all those who want a later start — wet, windy and bloody cold.

Our opening match in the five-team Benson and Hedges Cup group was against Derbyshire, and our entrance to

Ilkeston, shortly after breakfast time, was suitably startling. The convoy of Warwickshire Fiats, gaudily coloured, completed three circuits of the town roundabout as we tried to sort out directions to the ground. The Saturday shoppers leaped for their lives.

We needn't have rushed. Cricket before lunch was clearly out of the question. Looking at the soggy mess of a wicket, I remarked to England team-mate Geoff Miller that it was a bad drying ground. 'Not at all,' he said. 'It's just good at getting very wet!'

On wet mornings such as this, county cricketers are particularly adept at getting bored. Today, being day one of a new season, it seemed to catch everyone by surprise, and lost souls wandered aimlessly between dressing rooms, swapping stories and talking cricket.

Packer talk dominated, and Derbyshire's Mike Hendrick and Bob Taylor were soon in discussion with me over the recent Cricketers' Association meetings, which had left me pretty irritated. Various proposals had been filed, aimed at outlawing the Packer players from the English Test and first-class game, but they were subsequently not even voted upon, despite what I felt was a hardening attitude against Packer among most county players. Much more will be heard on this subject, I am quite sure.

Our own Kerry Packer player, 'Sacker' Amiss, seemed unmoved by the mounting feeling against him, even when someone suggested that he must have a brainwash tape from Packer inserted in the helmet that he now wears every time he goes out to bat.

Among the rest of the players, there is something different. It's noticeable that the spirit has improved; we seem a closer and happier unit, and I believe the new rules on team dress may have helped. From now on, we have a team dinner the night before each Bensons match, and everyone must wear blazers, collar and tie on the first day of each away game. It may sound nothing, but I'm sure it promotes a togetherness that had been missing before.

I took the lads out for some fielding practice, trying to mix up the routine of catches as much as possible to avert boredom. Someone still complained that it was too much to expect when we might be playing in mid-morning.

As it turned out, we got under way at 2.15 and Derbyshire enjoyed the afternoon more than we did. In the field first after losing the toss, we really didn't look a great side. Rebel had no rhythm, Art faded after a useful start, and Ernie was just Ernie . . . not very impressive. They made 220 and it could be enough.

Sunday April 23

Sometimes I wonder how I keep sane in this dressing room. Geoff Humpage arrived today in the worst pair of Union Jack socks I've ever seen, while Barnsley revolted us all with his regular wind problem after a few beers on Saturday night. To top it all, we were treated to the sight of Sacker marching out to bat complete with space-age helmet.

I am not against headgear. If the ball is flying off a wet pitch or a particularly hazardous one, I believe helmets can be a good idea both for safety and confidence. But I don't agree that they should be worn on slow pitches like this one.

I was right about 220 being enough. We never looked like challenging, and I was left with the deflating feeling that the one-day competitions are going to be a struggle for us again.

Monday April 24

At nine o'clock this morning, the committee room at Edgbaston began to fill up with players. The whole playing staff arrived for an inquest on yesterday's defeat – an innovation that must be a good thing so long as views are properly aired.

The captain had his say first, and my contribution was then to press for the use of six bowlers in the limited-overs games. With just the bare five we are in a mess as soon as someone so much as loses rhythm. Even the youngest players were encouraged to have their say, and I came out of the meeting an hour later feeling that something had been achieved.

An attempt at net practice was cut short by the perishingly cold weather. Three of the side have already started sniffing with colds, and I am fearful that the same could happen to me. Last season I had flu twice before we were properly under way.

A visit to Worcester to collect some kit from Duncan Fearnley, my bat maker and equipment supplier, put me behind schedule for the evening dinner at the Victoria Sporting Club, where Fiery was collecting a vanload of champagne for being the first man on the winter tour to score a century.

Traffic jams delayed me further, and I had to resort to changing into my suit in the Victoria car park. I had already missed the meal, though, and passed the rest of the evening chatting with selectors Charlie Elliott and Ken Barrington, and downing champagne. The chat was useful and I put over my dissatisfaction with some of the batsmen we had taken to Pakistan, who simply weren't up to Test standard. The champagne, I'm afraid, got me a little drunk.

Tuesday April 25
Hangover . . .

Wednesday April 26
Woke up in our Oxford hotel to a noise already familiar this

year . . . rain lashing against my bedroom window. We're due
to start a three-day friendly against the University today, but
as early as breakfast time the chances of any play seemed neg-
ligible.

Considering the weather, breakfast was a cheerful affair,
Smithy winning top prize with his totty-chasing memoirs of
the previous night. Having had no luck at all in his efforts
with the Oxfordshire ladies, he insisted that one would need
six O-Levels and three A-Levels to be allowed even chatting
time with them!

We arrived at The Parks startlingly smart in our new-
image, first-day uniform – until Barnsley arrived in second-
hand shirt, smelly jeans and suitably harassed expression telling the story of troubles down on his farm. The ground was
completely under water, so he could have stayed at home, and
after putting the lads through the regular training routine of
running, exercises and fielding practice, I opted to drive back
to Birmingham rather than hang about in Oxford.

Thursday April 27
The dreaded cold has struck me. Feel very ropey, even more so
as the weather continues foul and I made another fruitless
trek across country to Oxford. Last night's forecast predicted
snow and can only have been narrowly wrong – it is arctic.

Sympathize with Barnsley, who picked up a speeding ticket
en route from the farm to Oxford, and laugh at Art, the Kevin
Keegan of Scamps disco, all effort but no results, still getting
absolutely nowhere with the birds. Sleep then seems the most
inviting prospect and that is what I get.

Friday April 28
Miraculously, we have some cricket. Play was to start on time,

and as we were batting first, Barnsley and I escaped from the freezing, draughty wooden pavilion and slipped into Oxford just before the start. A spot of shopping, a hasty Wimpy with totty-spotting out of the window, then rush back to the ground in case we were 25 for 8. Although there were no such alarms, it was perhaps, on reflection, a rash thing to do for two senior players. The last thing I want is to encourage indiscipline among the young players; this time we were only persuaded to play truant by the bitter cold, our hunger and the fact that it was a relatively unimportant game.

Inevitably, and maybe mercifully, rain returned after lunch to draw the curtain over three forgettable days. Tomorrow brings our first home appearance of the season, against the amateurs of Minor Counties West in the Benson. It would not only be an embarrassment to lose this one but a disaster too, as we need to win our remaining three group games to qualify for the knockout stages.

Saturday April 29
Edgbaston is the most sought-after suburb of Birmingham. Nestling on the corner of a major junction, flanked by wide, tree-lined streets, stands the home of Warwickshire cricket, spacious, superbly built, well appointed – and generally empty. The people of Birmingham, it seems, would do anything to avoid their cricket team.

Today, the county's first home game of the season, it is emptier than usual. The weather is still uninviting, the opposition is unknown, and for once I honestly can't blame anyone for not shelling out their quid to come in.

Everything smells clean and scrubbed when I walk into the players' quarters and I find myself looking forward keenly to it all. Inside the dressing rooms, though, the archaic Warwickshire regulations remain to irritate us.

For some reason that dates back long before modern cricketers' habit of actually talking to each other, capped and
uncapped players are segregated at Warwickshire. The
uncapped guys have their own dressing room, naturally
smaller than the main one, and are also supposed to read a
player's card which tells them that they must knock before
entering the seniors' room and that if they are going to the
nets they must walk all around the main dressing room rather
than through it. Not my way of thinking, but it is still adhered
to relatively strictly at Edgbaston.

The rooms themselves are well equipped but faultily
designed. Tall lockers – two in the main room and one in the
juniors' – are fixed through the centre, placed so that if you sit
down you can see nobody on the other side of the room. Also,
there are two rows of pegs, the higher of which is out of reach
of everyone except me.

Green carpets cover a boarded floor which creaks in various
places, and most of the seats in the seniors' room are old armchairs which were supplied by the individual players of more
than a decade ago. Everyone has his own set place, and mine
happens to be next to a door which leads out to the players'
viewing area – a comfortable, glass-fronted terrace-type room
where we can sit and watch the cricket. Because of this, everyone seems fond of tripping over my feet or kicking my boots
whenever they come back into the dressing-room.

The luxury of the dressing-room used to be a television set,
but for this season it has been removed. It was decided by the
new regime that it was not a good thing to discourage players
from watching the play when we are batting, and a particularly bad thing to batsmen to have to walk into raucous laughter and general joviality from the TV viewers when they have
just been cleaned up.

This new rule deprived Barnsley and myself of the afternoon racing, as we dismissed the Minor Counties in no time

and strolled to a victory around teatime. These club players are simply not good enough in this company, and it may need a rethink over their inclusion in the competition. This was not an ideal game with which to kick off the Edgbaston season, as it was just too easy, and I remain unconvinced about our bowling strength when we meet more powerful opposition.

Sunday April 30
Heavy drizzle greeted my waking and I wondered if this weather would ever change. The thought of another fruitless journey, this time to Leicester, was far from appealing.

But somehow Leicester had escaped the elements, and our first John Player League fixture of the season got away on time. I was dismayed to find that the news of a prompt start brought on a general mood of despondency among our lads. We've got a poor record in the Sunday 40-over competition and an abysmal one against the champions, Leicester, but the attitude that two points for a washout beats none for a defeat is all wrong and must be sorted out.

Ray Illingworth put us in to bat, and we were dreadful. Yours truly scored 21 and that was the major effort in a total of 101. Leicester won without raising a sweat, and David Gower, the blond left-hander, impressed me greatly. He looks an England player.

The lads had never been at their chirpiest today, and the evening was positively sombre. We left Leicester without stopping for ale, choosing instead to do the sorrow-drowning back in Birmingham.

Monday May 1
With no cricket for two days, I have a chance to catch up on a lot of jobs. The first was accomplished this morning when I

visited a pal at Winits to be fitted with new boots. That may sound a simple task, but it's always a massive headache for me.

My left foot takes size $11\frac{1}{2}$ and my right foot size 11. The arch on my left foot has fallen, but not on my right. Both feet are narrow in body but splay at the toes. If you add all that together, it can be appreciated that any boot maker has troubles in creating the correct shape to support my feet and my strange, heavy bowling action. Nobody yet has completely succeeded.

Tuesday May 2

Report for nets, but that rain is falling again and practice outside is impossible. Apart from anything else, wet days are so expensive. I asked Art what he was planning for this afternoon and he replied: 'I'm cashing a cheque first.' I didn't cash any cheques but I did spend the afternoon with my accountant, trying to dream up ways to beat the taxman in a year where my earnings should profit considerably from commercial exposure. It's not on, though.

Indulged another of my sporting pleasures in the evening by going to watch the champions elect, Nottingham Forest, play West Bromwich Albion. I played a lot of soccer while I was playing for Surrey, and although cricket became an all-year-round career, my interest in the game never died.

Wednesday May 3

The fixture computer managed to slot a Championship game in amongst the jungle of limited-overs matches at the start of the season, but it couldn't counter the weather. It poured with rain all day, and the game against Surrey failed to start.

Several of the fellows from both sides departed into town

for lunch, but spent most of it arguing with a guy involved in a prang with Jasper. It doesn't seem to be Warwickshire's week for driving.

Thursday May 4
The first bridge school of the summer was set up today. Years ago, it was a regular thing for Sacker, John Jameson, Deryck Murray and Neal Abberley, but today Sacker struggled to find willing partners.

Surrey's players were split between backgammon and squash during the morning, but with none of the three appealing, I just ambled about for the morning session, looking forward to the 1000 Guineas race on television this afternoon.

Surprisingly, we started play at five o'clock – a one-innings game now – with Surrey batting first. After the close of play, most of us reported to the supporters' bar for a drink with the Surrey boys.

Friday May 5
Ours is the only game in England to escape the floods and resume, but it doesn't go the distance. After bowling quite well, we had plunged to 20 for 2 in no time at all when the rain bucketed down again.

I said my farewells to Surrey's Geoff Howarth, who spent a winter living with me at my parents' place when he first came over from New Zealand, before setting off for a celebratory Chinese meal, Barnsley, Jasper and myself having scooped £360 on the afternoon's racing.

Saturday and Sunday May 6 and 7
A weekend of doing next to nothing, and I enjoyed every

minute. It's our Saturday off on the Benson and Hedges rota, and I spent it at the races with Barnsley. On the way back, he collected his second speeding ticket in ten days. After several minutes of bleak silence, Barnsley killed the atmosphere by wondering aloud whether the Thames Valley Police might invite him to their annual dinner and present him with the mounted steering-wheel if he got the hat-trick.

Monday May 8

Coventry's Courtaulds ground will never win any prizes for beauty. It is a soul-destroying place to play cricket, and today, with the steel-grey skies matching the surrounds, it was doubly dismal. A victory cheers up any cricketer, however, and this was one we badly needed. We scored just 200 and I feared it might not be enough to defend in a 55-over Bensons game against a side with as many potential big-innings men as Lancashire.

Our cause was not helped by two things: Humpty is still hobbling on one leg, not really fit and finding keeping wicket difficult, and when we thought big Clive 'Hubert' Lloyd was out once, he didn't think so. Finally and ironically, Humpty stumped Hubert off The Whale at a critical stage, which virtually killed Lancashire's chances.

Barnsley got the man-of-the-match award for three cheap wickets and we spent the evening consoling some pretty depressed Lancashire players.

Tuesday May 9

Flight gave me the day off today, but it is important that I show the right attitude, so I turned up at the ground to do

some supervising of nets and push myself through twenty laps
of the Colts ground.

Wednesday May 10
Yorkshire are at Edgbaston for a three-day game, and the
weather is better at last. Sacker rose to the occasion with his
first century of the season, and we topped 300, but in the
evening session Geoff Boycott made it perfectly plain that
nothing less than three figures will do for him tomorrow. A
hundred looks inevitable.

Alec Bedser, chairman of England's selectors, was here
today to take the pressure off Mike Brearley by informing
Boycott that he was not going to be captain against Pakistan.
Mike's re-appointment will meet with the approval of every
England player.

The evening social venue was moved tonight. Fed up with
some of the comments in the Supporters' Bar, the players'
camp has moved to the White Swan, a large, welcoming pub
and steak bar about a mile from the ground and conveniently
closer to my new house in Edgbaston. I had conducted negotiations with the landlord to lay the ground for regular
invasions of thirsty cricketers, and first impressions were good
all round.

Thursday May 11
Boycott duly completed his century and I spent the day flog-
ging without hope against a dead wicket. I'm becoming ever
more convinced that the current Championship rules are
hopeless. The 100-over limit on first-innings turns almost
every game into three one-day slogs. Only the first three or
four in each side have the chance to bat properly, and that
must be bad for the game.

Smithy let me down tonight. I've spent hours fighting for

him to open the batting, but he got himself out to a dreadful shot against Geoff Cope and won himself a rollicking from me.

Drama by night as I locked myself out of my house and my car, leaving the keys in the house as I slammed the door. I was almost resigned to kipping on the pavement when I remembered Big Sue, the girl who does my laundry, and woke her to beg the spare bed.

Friday May 12

An amazing day's cricket left us with an unexpected and spectacular victory.

We continued to collapse and left Yorkshire to make only 145 to win, on a pitch as placid as any we will see this season. Unharmed by my disturbed night, however, I took the highly satisfying scalp of Boycott for just four, and the rest fell apart to Barnsley and myself. This was the answer to a few prayers at this stage of the season, and although it is too early for sweeping statements, it does at least seem that our optimism was not entirely misplaced.

Celebrated in style with supper at a favourite eating establishment, called The Towrope. On the surface, it is no more than a transport cafe, but inside they serve good cheap grub in the sort of atmosphere that makes your hair curl. Gets a few stars in the Willis guide to eating out.

Saturday May 13

Our second successive Saturday off, and one that we could have done without now that we have established momentum with a couple of wins. A quiet day, concluded by a meal with Derrick Robins, a much-maligned man who does a great deal for cricket and cricketers, even if he does dominate conversations! Without him, many county players would never have been on a tour, and it was on this subject that he sought an audience with me. Derrick is currently negotiating to take a party to Rhodesia in September and wants me to get involved. Needs some thought, with so little time between the end of the season and the Australian tour.

Sunday May 14
Kent have never been my favourite bunch of blokes and I liked them even less when they beat us today in the Sunday League. We didn't make enough runs again, but we had them in a lot of bother until John Shepherd saw them home. So, another John Player defeat and a fairly gloomy evening drink with 'Deadly' Underwood, who is one of my great mates, and some of the other Kent guys.

*   *   *

Friday May 19
Five successive days without cricket end today. Relaxing it may be, but sensible it certainly isn't. What we need at the start of the season is a lot of cricket together, not the totally disjointed opening that the Benson and Hedges Cup programme provides. There is a lot of talk among the players that the format should be changed and the season opened by a series of three-day matches. I must go along with that, although I must say I enjoyed the rest.

At lunchtime today, a party of us set off early for tomorrow's crucial Benson match at Bristol, stopping off at a rather special country house hotel near Cheltenham, Bibury Court. The match against Gloucestershire will decide our fate in this competition, and confidence grew with every mouthful of champagne on the sun-drenched terrace. It was an idyllic afternoon, and when we reached Bristol, Barnsley was anxious to complete it in style. Slinging his golf bags over his shoulder, he marched purposefully into the Avon Gorge Hotel – and fell down the steps. . . . The team dinner was noisy and exuberant, and I think we are in the mood to win.

Saturday May 20

Alvin Kallicharran is back with us after captaining the West Indies, following the walk-out of their Packer players, against Australia. The aftermath of the series is clearly affecting him – he too had signed for Packer but obtained release last year – but on today's evidence it is certainly not harming his form. He scored a brilliant 107 out of 234, and after some moments of concern while Mike Procter was in, we defeated Gloucester comfortably to enter the last eight.

Into each life . . . a group of very undesirable apparent Warwickshire followers – I refuse to term them supporters – accosted us in the Bristol bar. Quite honestly the club would be better off without people like these.

Sunday May 21

After journeying overnight to Poole for a stop with Barnsley's in-laws, we dallied at Parkstone Yacht Club this morning and left a little behind schedule, and a little reluctantly, for the week's John Player League game at Southampton.

My routine of exercises is now being adopted religiously, which is good to see, but today, as on most other Sundays, it made little difference. Hampshire scored 230-plus and we were never in it.

Barnsley was hit for 63 in his eight overs, and with all respect he should have been off. We must manipulate the bowlers better and use all six available to us.

Monday May 22
For the first time ever, the Benson and Hedges Cup draw is broadcast live on the radio, and it makes compulsive listening. We are at home to Glamorgan, and that suits me fine. I'm really pleased with our efforts in the Benson, although the comparison with our Sunday disasters is almost beyond belief.

Tuesday May 23
After a long discussion, the selection committee finally agreed that Smithy could bat first against Leicestershire tomorrow — much to my satisfaction. With that done, my thoughts moved elsewhere. This is where I leave the county scene for the first time this summer and begin the international season. Tomorrow we play the first one-day Prudential International against Pakistan at Manchester, and already the familiar signs of nerves are beginning to bite. Back with the England boys — and it hardly seems five minutes ago that we were in New Zealand.

2
Hero and Villain

Tuesday May 23 continued

Geoff Boycott is not a naturally humorous man. Those who expect streams of witticisms would be disappointed by him. He takes himself as seriously as he takes his cricket, and apart from the occasional dry comment, life is seldom other than a solemn business. He is selfish on the field, self-indulgent in most ways and possesses the unfortunate knack of saying the wrong thing. He provokes more fervent emotions, both pro and anti, than any other cricketer of my time.

But I can't help admiring him. Fiery's knowledge of the game, and his recollection of individual events on the field, are quite unsurpassed, and any player who gives him a chance will learn a great deal from what he has to say.

At social events, however, he is often a figure apart. He seldom drinks to excess, nor does his conversation often veer far from cricket topics. But be that as it may, I can think of nobody less likely to commit the gaffe he perpetrated to-night . . .

As usual, the selectors had attended the team dinner, which on this occasion was staged at the Mottram Hall Hotel. The hottest news for us all was that poor Scagg had injured his finger and Fiery, declaring himself recovered from his own troublesome ailments, will take over as captain.

Alec Bedser made his ritual speech and told us that he wanted the one-day internationals used as preliminaries to the Test series; we weren't to worry too much about winning. There are two reasons, however, why we shall worry a good deal about winning: victory will give us a psychological advantage for the more serious business ahead, and it's also worth a lot of cash.

When the selectors left us, the talk relaxed into chat about players around the country who have impressed us, something that happens all the time when cricketers get together. We then reverted to tomorrow's match and began to dissect the opposition, player by player. Each of the Pakistanis' strengths and weaknesses were discussed, something that was not difficult for most of us who had been on the winter tour there.

It was midway through this debate that Fiery brought the house down. Becoming quite intense, he informed us all that Shafiq was often suspect to the hook shot.

Nobody had told him that Shafiq was not even on the tour.

Wednesday May 24

Not a pleasant morning to start the international season. My first thought as I poked my head through the hotel curtains was that the match would not finish today, and, although the threatened rain stayed away, so it was to prove.

Hendo and JK were the unlucky ones left out when we chose eleven from thirteen — God knows they have both suffered that fate enough over recent series. Fiery won the toss and chose to bat in pretty indifferent light. Within minutes, he was out himself for only three, and such is the importance of the man to our side that I felt we were immediately in trouble.

The pressure was intense on Clive Radley and Barry

Wood. Neither can be sure of a place in the Tests, but both are pastmasters at the limited-overs innings, and after cautious beginnings they began to flourish. David Gower looked good in his first match of any sort for England, but he must stop wafting at the ball outside off stump if he gets a chance in the Test side. At this level, it will get him out more often than not.

We finished with 217, which was a reasonable effort in unfavourable batting conditions, but so much time was lost to bad light that we had only an hour at them in the evening. I felt a bit rusty as I ran in; nothing fundamentally wrong, but enough for me to notice. I couldn't be displeased, though, as I got rid of Sadiq, so often the danger man. Chilly bowled tightly at the other end, and I think we are in a healthy position to win this one.

After close of play, I turned up at the Prudential reception for players and guests, more out of courtesy than enthusiasm. Tomorrow's bowling occupied my thoughts, and after a quiet meal it was early to bed.

Thursday May 25
There are times in this game when all the sweating, fretting, even the planning, seems overdone and unnecessary. Today was just such an occasion. Pakistan, whom we had credited with a number of highly talented players, collapsed pitifully to 30 for 7 and were ultimately all out for around 60.

Yours truly returned 4 for 15 in eleven overs and picked up the 'Man of the Match' award. The rhythm was there today, and the speed too. It was a thrill just to be doing well again at international level, albeit in a limited-over match, but as it finished I wondered if this really provided an omen for the series ahead or if it is no more than a one-off disaster for the Pakistanis.

JK was my car mate for the long haul down the M6 and M1 to London for tomorrow's second international at The Oval. As ever when cricketers get together, our chatter was chiefly about cricketers. But we also deliberated on our chances of holidaying together in the States when the season is over. I fear there may be just too little time.

Friday May 26
How do you feel when you wake up to be told that you are captain of England — if only for a day? That was my unexpected privilege this morning, following Fiery's sudden withdrawal with a thumb injury.

I've captained the side before, but only in New Zealand. This, before an English crowd and on the ground where I began my career, seemed different . . . more significant, more stimulating.

Alone in the Great Western Hotel, after being given the news, my thoughts were dominated by the toss. Oval pitches are so flat and benign that I felt we must win it, bat well and set them a target as close to unassailable as it is possible to get.

The first wish was rejected — I lost the toss. But amazingly, for no reason that I could fathom, Pakistan's captain Wasim Bari put us in to bat. David Gower made a marvellous unbeaten century and my target of 260 was realized. This time, we didn't bowl Pakistan out, but the result was still never in doubt. They made so little effort it was almost embarrassing, and I even brought on one or two joke bowlers at the end, more to keep the crowd amused than anything.

Tonight, the Pru's reception seemed a brighter affair. Tannoy and Grummidge and the rest of the family were there, proud of their boy I hope, but the reunion was all too brief and I was soon heading back up the motorway to Birmingham with England physio Bernard Thomas, complete with brand-new MGB GT.

As the car was still being run in and the drive more a crawl than a dash, I had plenty of time to chat with Bernard, and to appreciate once again what an important part he has had to play in my life, and the lives of so many cricketers.

I recall exactly when I met him first. It was November 22, 1970, the day that I arrived in Australia as a fresh-faced twenty-one-year-old, having been summoned to join the England tour as replacement for the injured Alan Ward. I checked in at the Park Royal Hotel in Brisbane at seven in the morning, but Bernard was up to meet me and supervise my needs after a gruelling flight. He helped me through the problems of that first England tour and was then instrumental in my move from Surrey, where I was desperately unsettled, to Warwickshire, where he had long been physiotherapist.

We have been close friends ever since that tour, and it is Bernard who got me thinking positively about injuries at a time when I was almost resigned to them finishing my career. He made me realize that just because I felt a pain, it did not mean it would get worse if I played with it. The greatest example was in Melbourne in 1971, when I was struggling with a shoulder strain. Bernard assured me that I would be in agony for my first three deliveries and it would then get better. He was right; at first I could hardly get my arm over, but the pain quickly disappeared completely.

Officially, Bernard's job is to tend the injuries in the Warwickshire and England camp. He attends every day of every Warwickshire home game from before the start until lunchtime, and is always available to us in his huge and impressive health clinic at Edgbaston. But to the England side on tour, he is much more than a physio. He is father confessor, nurse-maid, a friend to all who need him. I have known him to be turfed out of bed at all hours of the night, especially in India and Pakistan, with players vomiting on his floor, stricken with food poisoning.

He advises on any sort of problem any of the players may encounter – and does it in confidence. He is astute enough to do the right thing at a boring reception, and round up the players as soon as courtesy allows it. He also saved the life of New Zealand's Ewan Chatfield when he was hit on the head by Peter Lever in 1971, an incident I shall never be able to forget.

So at the end of a mad week in which my cricket route has been Birmingham—Bristol—Southampton—Birmingham —Manchester—London—Birmingham, I was pleased to spend some time with Bernard, and watch the TV highlights of my day as captain back at his house. A very good day, indeed.

Saturday May 27

The danger of this account is that I am likely to repeat myself occasionally, and there is no subject on which I am more prone to grow tedious than that of the Championship regulations. Yet again, at Worcester today, I was frustrated by that rule which restricts the first innings to 100 overs per side. It has made the Championship too predictable; every day is beginning to seem the same.

My patience and temper with the situation were not helped by my physical condition, which after the rigours of the past week is approaching complete fatigue before we have even begun the Test series. I feel as though I need a week's sleep. A day in the field was just what I didn't need today. Barnsley was back in the side after injury, but our problems are growing rather than being solved. I think we have a crisis of confidence among some of the players.

Rebel was left out today and Russell Flower was given another game. But by mid-afternoon, our massed spin strength of Flower-Power and Eddie The Whale looked something less than terrifying. Worcester obviously thought so, and a shaky 90 for 5 became a total of some respect by the close of the innings.

Sunday May 28
Sunday now has a new name in the Warwickshire dressing room – the Black Sabbath.

This particular sabbath provided our fourth John Player League defeat in four attempts. We're so bad at this game it's difficult to know whether to laugh or cry; it's even more difficult to see us missing out on the wooden spoon unless we make a dramatic improvement.

It was a bad day all round, although it began pleasantly enough with breakfast 100 yards up the road at Jim Cumbes' house – yes, dining with the opposition – before setting off for Worcester and the delights of the 40-over thrash. Injuries gave us some excuse – Whale and Kalli were both missing – but after keeping them down to 177 we should at least have been in with a shout. But no, we batted abysmally yet again.

A dreadful Worcestershire supporters' shindig deepened my depression until I managed to escape back to my pit, determined to catch as much sleep as possible with the first Test looming up rapidly.

Monday May 29
Glenn Turner and I were involved in the kind of pantomime today that seems a momentary diversion at the time, but which is invariably transformed into a 'shock-horror-storm' by the press. I doubt whether this one will be any exception.

Glenn opens for Worcester. He comes from New Zealand and is easily his country's best batsman, but he has declined to play on their tour of England this summer, preferring to concentrate on his benefit.

The incident was fired by my conviction that Glenn doesn't play the bouncer too well. Consequently I gave him a few. He was neither pleased nor comfortable, so the treatment was repeated. At that point, Glenn made something of a charade of calling for Sacker's helmet, which was duly brought out to him. I delivered one more ball, and as he looked for another bouncer, had him lbw playing back. That, I imagined, was the end of the episode.

But back in the dressing room, Glenn — maybe in the heat of the moment — let off steam to the press and claimed that I should have been warned for persistent use of the short ball. I was asked for a quote later, and I had to say I couldn't understand what he was complaining about. God protect us from the day when fast bowlers are so shackled that they cannot use the weapon of the bouncer against so-called class batsmen!

That was the unpleasant flashpoint of another bad day for Warwickshire. We're not playing well, that's all there is to it, and one of our major weaknesses is in the spin-bowling department. Elvis is still bowling as he would in club cricket, and Eddie just doesn't have enough control.

The one happy event of the day was provided by a member of the opposition. Jim Cumbes was capped at last, after fifteen years of wandering among the counties. It called for a celebration of course, and the host beamed in honest and obvious pleasure at his own barbecue. I feel very very pleased for him tonight. He'll never be a great cricketer, but he'll also never be less than useful. And apart from that, he's one of my best mates!

Tuesday May 30
On the field at Worcester, we were set about 300 in plenty of time, but after Sacker and Smithy had given us a good start, a

pack-of-cards collapse gave us no option but to play for the draw.

The day echoed to the sound of Barnsley's grumbles, having heard that Barry Richards, in his new book, was proposing that cricketers over thirty-five should take a drop in wages and be phased out as they were no longer of use to the game. D. J. Brown, at thirty-six years of age, didn't agree.

Talking of age, it's my twenty-ninth birthday. Many more, and I will qualify for one of the most dreaded adjectives in cricket – veteran. I threw a party of my own tonight, and although the attendance was a conservative thirty, it was a success. The evening's merriments were not too protracted, and I was in bed by one in the morning with the thought that the Test was less than thirty-six hours away, and the butterflies considerably closer.

3
The First Test against Pakistan

Wednesday May 31

There is a ritual feel about the eve of a Test match. It may not necessarily be looked forward to; the nervous may dread it. But nobody questions the value of what we are asked to do.

Today was the first such day of the summer, and consequently carried the most stress. My stomach was unsettled as soon as I got up – and that wasn't last night's alcohol. I spent the morning washing up the debris from the party, tidying the house, anything to keep my mind and body active.

At two o'clock, I left for Edgbaston. The ritual had begun. Birthday cards and letters had arrived for me in some numbers, and I filled in time reading them – some amusing, some touching, some just stupid – until the rest of the side began to arrive.

A glance around the faces was fascinating, as I took my usual Warwickshire place in the dressing room. Some of the lads showed clear signs of edginess, yet David Gower, selected for his first Test at an age rarely risked in this country, looked totally unmoved. I have to wonder if that is a good thing, but then we are all made up so differently that it would be wrong of me to judge anyone else on my emotional standards.

The dressing room talk was of the increasing number of people – batsmen and fielders – who are being hit on the head, and of protective helmets. Sacker, who is marketing the things, was there with a pile of order forms, and he reports that the current rate of acceptance is about four helmets per county. Good business.

My clash with Glenn Turner was also a popular topic. The papers, as expected, had built it up into a confrontation, and I can't blame them for that, as bouncers are the great talking point right now.

By shortly after three, we were all in the nets, Fiery receiving only a few balls before declaring that his thumb was still too sore to contemplate playing. His present poor form, unusually studded with low scores, would not have helped him any in deciding to play, and already the vultures are crowding him with conjecture that he is psyching himself out of Test cricket, just as he did in 1974. It may be so, but I prefer to give him a better chance than that.

Something was not quite right in the dressing room. It wasn't much, and perhaps I've been spoiled by the unbelievably good spirit that has been maintained since the tour of India four years ago, but I'm sure we weren't quite so happy. It's hard to define, this hint of slightly less camaraderie, and the one reason I can think of is that John Lever is not playing.

We miss JK badly, there can be no doubt about that. He is a very talented and essentially international bowler – a great performer all round the world. He is unlucky not to get in the side, for he is more than an on-field contributor. Off the pitch, in dressing rooms and hotels, he is a character, a cheerful and amusing guy who lifts morale by his sheer presence. I hope he will be back soon.

With nets over, I wandered out to the middle with Scagg to inspect the wicket. It looks firmer than most at Edgbaston, but that should just make it better than ever for the batsmen. It might go through more quickly than is customary at the start, but the ball will be coming onto the bat – I can't see there being a lot in it for me. At this stage, however, I still thought we would probably play all four of our seam bowlers and omit a spinner, as Pakistan are notoriously weak against top-class fast bowling.

I slipped home briefly after that, my house being only a couple of minutes' drive from the ground, but by seven I was at the Albany Hotel in town for the pre-match dinner; a further part of the ritual.

As usual, we gathered in the bar, and the first people I came across were Alec Bedser and David Gower, very much the old hand and the rookie. Alec was earnestly extolling the virtues of playing straight; I hope David heeds his advice.

Inside the dining room, the big eaters got stuck in, Both and Chilly demolishing as much as the establishment could put before them. Alec stood up at the end and made his patriotic speech, adding how delighted he was that we were all so smartly turned out. Dress is a very big thing with Alec, and I think he's right. In that sense, I am old-fashioned enough to appreciate that the feeling of togetherness which is so important to any team can only be improved by a smart uniform.

As is customary, the selectors left at this point, and the team were free to talk amongst themselves. Our first communal conversation point was how the prize money should be split; it's a considerable amount this year, under the Cornhill sponsorship, and we agreed that the twelfth man must be cut in on everything.

Just as we had before the one-day games, we talked through the Pakistani batsmen, and this time Fiery negotiated the discussion without a blunder! The one batsman we struggled to sort out was Sarfraz. He may come in as low as number eight or nine, but personally I find him a pest to bowl at. His reach, like mine, is so extensive that he persistently hits good-length deliveries through the off side as if they were half-volleys.

As the dinner began to break up, Scagg asked Fiery, Chilly,

Bob 'Chat' and myself to stay behind, and asked our opinions on selection. Despite my earlier thoughts that the Pakistanis were vulnerable against seam, it now looks as if we will opt for greater balance and play Dusty Miller as the extra spinner. So poor old Hendo will miss out again.

While the rest of the lads wended their way up to their hotel rooms, I went home, preferring the comforts of my own bed and surroundings on the night that stretches my nerve-ends more than any other in a season.

Thursday June 1

Sleep is elusive, and trying to sleep just irritating, so I'm up early. The guts are turning over quite violently, but I would be more worried if they weren't. The nerves have become part of my own ritual, and if they don't make themselves known, something must be wrong.

I'm not good company on mornings like this and I prefer being alone with my thoughts and my shakes. Those who don't know me would probably never suspect that I suffer from nerves like this. It's at its worst on the first day of a Test, and particularly the first Test. Today, perhaps, it is still more acute because for me it is a home Test. There are more people to let down when you play at home.

Outside, it is bright and sunny. But it rained overnight, and there is still the hint of a storm in the air. That could prove interesting later.

After just a few minutes of pacing I turn for comfort to my stereo, and the music of Bob Dylan. He can be soothing as well as stimulating; just as Scagg hums a Rasoumovsky cello passage to himself when batting, I can sing Dylan in my mind to divert my brain from what is to come. I've been known to imitate him rather more demonstratively, too!

The ground beckons earlier than usual. I can't stand

hanging about at home any longer, and anyway, this being a home Test, I've got problems trying to sort out enough tickets to keep the friends and relatives happy. Our allowance this year has been increased from two to four per day, but I still have to beg a few from the other lads.

The dressing room, as ever before a match, is a base for a good deal of pretence and bravado. Many like to make it seem that they are not nervous; I never bother to hide it. Generally, I'm too involved in my own feelings to study those of the others, but today I made the effort to look around.

Mike is quiet, but then that isn't unusual. A deep man, Scagg, and although I count him as one of my few really close friends in the game, I find it hard to know how much his nerves affect him.

Gower looks no different to yesterday. You would never have put him down as a youngster playing in his first Test. I don't think Both suffers much, nor Philip Edmonds. Chilly perhaps looks a little paler than usual. Rad and Dusty are pretty subdued.

It's a relief to get out on the pitch. Almost ninety minutes remain before the start, but the seats are beginning to fill. The sun by now is blazing – it's getting hotter by the minute.

I bowled a few balls at Bob 'Chat' Taylor just to get myself loose, then went through my exercise routine with our physio, Bernard Thomas. One of the stretches involves me putting my legs on Bernie's shoulders – one at a time. It's not quite as difficult as it sounds, because Bernie is about a foot shorter than me, but it made such an odd sight that the cameramen latched onto it straight away.

The captains tossed early, fifty minutes before the start. Wasim Bari won it and made the natural choice to bat first, so I had three quarters of an hour to build myself up to bowling. Instead of improving, the nerves got steadily worse, only easing as I burst out from behind the captain and sprinted onto the ground at 11.25. That part has become habit since the time of Tony Greig as captain; at one time there were about six of us in the side who would sprint past the captain, fanning out into a pattern. It might upset the theorists, but it does release some of the tension.

I feel better as soon as the first over is past. The tension eases quite noticeably. Chris Old bowls from the pavilion end, as tidily and competently as ever, but from the other end I find it hard to collect my rhythm. I know things are not quite right.

Before lunch, we picked up two fairly fortunate wickets, and during the break it was decided that I should switch ends for another burst. The change worked marvellously. Suddenly, the punch and the tempo was back in my bowling, and the pace naturally followed. Three good bouncers began to sort out the Pakistan weakness. Mohsin Khan was taken aback by the first and dismissed by the second; the third accounted for Haroon. Those who say bouncers are not part of the game should have been here today – the crowd loved it, too.

But my achievements paled against those of Chilly, now operating from the end where I began the day. He enjoyed the sort of over that comes to each of us once in a lifetime . . . if we are lucky. It was a dream that he should remember for the rest of his life. Four wickets fell to him in the space of five deliveries; the one he failed with was a no-ball. The cloud cover certainly helped him, but he earned the success with his great line and length.

Suddenly, Pakistan were on their backs. We had cut into the soft underbelly of their batting and I think they may not recover. It's true that they have several very talented players, but in our conditions and against the quality of bowling that we can boast at the moment, I can see them struggling for a big score.

They were reprieved tonight only by bad light, which cut

into the game with nine wickets down. We could scarcely complain; it has been a terrific first day of the series for us, and we are already in a position where victory is beckoning.

Sometimes, after a really good day on the field, the evening's socializing can seem a dreadful anticlimax. It was that way tonight. I made only a token appearance at the reception thrown by our friendly sponsors, Cornhill.

The White Swan provided a haven, and along with Chilly – smug smile a fixture as he accepted pints from enthusiastic admirers of his day's bowling – I began to relax at last. I was even able to laugh at the state I had got into before the game; when success comes as simply as it did today, I wonder why I worry!

Some of our Warwickshire second team lads were in the pub and I made a mental note to persuade the committee that they must sign Chris Clifford – an experienced spinner recommended to us by Geoff Boycott – as replacement for Eddie Hemmings, who may need surgery on his injured knee.

I can't completely cut myself off from the county scene at any time, but tonight England is what matters to me. I'm confident now that we have the bowling weapons to win the series – and I'm far more assured about the prospect of Radley and Gower batting for us tomorrow than I was about one or two who played in the Tests on tour last winter.

Friday June 2
Some people are born to be Test cricketers; on today's evidence, David Gower is one of the lucky few. His first scoring shot was an arrogant hook for four; he had one lucky escape and went on to play like a young master, an innings full of beautiful shots. A lot of people are going to travel a long way to watch this fellow bat in years to come.

David's success was just one of the good points in another

excellent day for us. It was a day on which I didn't have to set foot on the ground after the first few minutes – the time it took Chilly to roll over their last man, Liaquat Ali – but I still ended it feeling desperately tired.

My problem in life is that I very rarely sleep well. It's much worse at Test match time, and I think maybe this year has been worse than ever before. I just toss and turn at nights. I can seldom sleep at all after about six in the morning, and, once awake, I'm not one for lying around in bed.

It was the same this morning. My father stayed at home last night and we were both up early. Reading the papers, eating a sparse breakfast, playing some more Dylan music . . . then down to the ground by 10.15 a.m. for another bout of handing out tickets, exercising and netting.

After we had taken the final Pakistan wicket, Scagg and Barry Wood – whose selection surprised me greatly – went into conference in the dressing room. The captain, not sure of Woody's preferences, asked, 'What about the first ball?' Mike Hendrick, from the other side of the room, intervened with his broad Derbyshire Dales accent, 'Hit the bloody thing for six!'

Our fortune continued to hold; Sarfraz, the one Pakistan seamer who would normally cause us much real concern, went off injured early in the afternoon, and didn't return for the rest of the day. But although everything was running with re-markable smoothness, I still can't fully wind down.

I'm edgy and fidgety in the dressing room. Whereas some of the lads can turn off completely – Phil Edmonds has a sleep, several others play cards – I'm a permanent wanderer. I can't even sit and watch the game for long. I'm probably the worst spectator in the world. I don't want to bowl again too soon, be-cause I need time to recover energy, so I'm desperately hoping that the batsmen do well.

They didn't let me down. Woody went early, which seemed

to amplify my doubts over his initial selection, but Scagg and
Rad went well until the captain ran himself out. He thought
he had got in, but confessed it was a foolish run to attempt.

Then there was Gower, and at this stage I won't swamp him
with any more praise that may turn out – though I don't think
so – to have been premature.

To be frank, their bowling was pretty ropey. Qasim, whose
left-arm spin was one of their most potent weapons last
winter, bowled badly for most of the day, and I feel they may
be sunk without trace if we keep them in the field for another
full day.

I used up a good part of the afternoon by changing horses
back to being a Warwickshire player again. The chairman of
the cricket committee, Mike Smith, John Whitehouse, Alan
Oakman and myself got together for what was to be a very important meeting. I was unhappy with the views of MJK and
Flight: I want positive steps now to establish Dennis Amiss's
future, get the young players involved and line up a replacement for Rohan Kanhai. The coach, I feel, is on my side, but a
confrontation could be looming . . . not a pleasant thought to
end another very pleasant day for England.

Saturday June 3
Just what I needed – I was woken from a deep sleep, in the
middle of the night, by the ring of the telephone. It was a
former girlfriend, stoned out of her mind. Needless to say, it
didn't help my sleep problems, and the rest of the night passed
desperately slowly.

But there was plenty to be pleased about slightly later in the
day. Rad battled on to a typical hundred, and by being the
first England centurion of the series he won a hundred bottles
of champagne. For the crowd, however, the best enter-
tainment came from Ian Botham, now nicknamed 'the Master

Butcher' by Phil Edmonds and myself as a tribute to his batting style.

The Butcher carved the attack into tiny pieces and ate them for breakfast in a century as devastating as any I've seen in recent times. It can't rank with the best, because the bowling was by then so demoralized, but to have a fellow like this coming in at number seven is the ideal bonus for any captain.

Roope and Miller both made runs, but I can't help a repetition of the niggling suspicions that I had about them during the winter tour – that neither man is quite good enough for the top flight. While watching them, I chatted lengthily with Scagg about county cricket, the possibility of four-day matches, wicket covers and players who might challenge for an England place. But yet again we got back to names such as Keith Fletcher, Frank Hayes and Alan Jones – all fine players, but at their age, hardly progressive steps.

We had barely finished talking when Mike declared, which upset me considerably. I thought we ought to keep the Pakistanis out there just as long as we could; grind them into the dust. Mike, who was having second thoughts about the choice of Dusty in preference to Hendo, felt that we ought to get at them again.

By the end of the day, they had reached 100 with only one wicket down, but Edmonds – 'Henry' or 'Goat' to us all – turned a few deliveries in the last half-hour, enough to give us real hope that we would finish the job.

I had bowled below my best, and in searching for a reason I found that there was a distinct lack of atmosphere in the ground. The crowd was a fair size, but nowhere near as big as a Saturday of the first Test should produce. Everyone at Edgbaston must be disappointed.

Saturday night fever got to me. It is always the first and only time I let myself go during a Test match, and with no play the next morning I generally have a good night. Tonight I visited various boozeries with the Master Butcher, finally watching the World Cup and the Test highlights through an alcoholic haze and retiring to the luxuries of The Towrope for a 75p *à la carte* dinner.

Sunday June 4

Music and fresh air relaxes me and clears my head. With the french windows flung open, and Dylan once again playing on the stereo, I feel more at peace with the world than at any time for a week.

My mother and father were at home for the day, and I was rather looking forward to twenty-four hours of doing nothing before returning to the battle front tomorrow. The best-laid plans rarely come to fruition, though, and this was a case in point. In mid-morning, a telephone call brought the disturbing news that a great pal of mine had slipped back into alcoholism trouble. It had happened before, but it didn't ease my distress for a very genuine friend. A group of us went round to his house in the afternoon and gave him the hard line – that if he didn't stop drinking, he would lose everything.

Monday June 5

Controversy has always tended to follow the fast bowlers around. Today it was my turn, and I didn't enjoy the experience.

The story in its crudest form is that I hit Pakistan's nightwatchman, Iqbal Qasim, in the face with a bouncer and made quite a mess of him. The press appear to be turning it into a full-blown scandal, suggesting in some cases that I deliberately set out to hit the fellow, and in others that Scagg should apologize on my behalf. The Pakistanis are furious and are threatening to complain to Lord's about it.

Personally, I think it's all been exaggerated nonsensically – and that does not mean that I'm callous enough to have no feelings for the batsman who got hurt. There are bowlers around, Dennis Lillee and Jeff Thomson among them, who have caused a considerable stir by stating publicly that they occasionally bowl with intent to injure. I would never like that to be said of me, because I get no pleasure at all from the sight of anyone being hit in the face, particularly when I am the bowler.

Just once in my career, temper got the better of me to a dangerous extent. It was in 1972 and the batsman was Barry Wood, ironically an England team-mate here. Woody was walking down the wicket to play me on a very flat and lifeless Edgbaston wicket, and I became so riled that I bowled him a beamer, actually wanting it to hit him. Luckily for me, the ball only glanced off his glove. I think I realized in a matter of seconds what a stupid reaction that was, and since then my intentions have always been to get batsmen out – frighten them maybe, but never physically hurt them.

I'm not in the habit of bowling bouncers at tailenders either, but today was a special case. Qasim came in at number three on Saturday evening, and hung around for another forty minutes this morning. By that stage, I considered he had qualified for a little softening up. I bowled him three bouncers over a period. The first two he avoided, the third he made an ineffectual attempt to duck, and deflected the ball into his mouth. The sound was sickening and the sight almost as bad. Blood ran fairly freely while most of our fielders clustered around Qasim to lend what assistance they could. I stayed back, not because I didn't care but because I need to keep detached when batsmen are hurt.

Qasim went off to hospital for a stitching operation, and didn't resume his innings. We winkled out the rest fairly smartly after lunch, and completed an innings win around teatime – a victory that was soured just a little for me.

The after-match champagne tasted a bit flat; I was tired and hungry, and the news that several of the national newspaper 'hatchet-men' wanted to see me for a quote on Qasim did little to improve my mood. I said nothing to them, and simply couldn't understand the fuss. It upset me, nevertheless.

From one disturbance to another . . . two drunken supporters in the social club were causing a menace, so I bundled them into the car and took them home. The good deed done, I retired to the White Swan with a few friends, anxious to get away from accusing eyes and just as anxious to get some sleep.

Tuesday June 6

Newspaper reaction to yesterday's incident is severe, almost hysterical, and fairly unanimous in condemnation of me. I can report this only because I have been told about it, as I have got into the habit of simply not reading papers; subconsciously cutting myself off. I'm a little ashamed to admit this, as I believe I probably should read them, if only to keep up on the news of the world and the news on the cricket scene. It stems, though, from being upset several times in the past by articles that I have considered to be unfair. I don't want to be upset again, so I'd prefer not to know the worst. Today I could hardly avoid it, even by studiously ignoring every newspaper in sight!

The morning passed peacefully enough, drawing a raffle at Edgbaston, and after a few exercises I felt tired again. I'm not sleeping well, and last night was one of my worst for some while. This afternoon I settled down in front of the television and dozed; the World Cup football failed to grab me and I was happy to get an early night.

4
The Second Test against Pakistan

Wednesday June 7

There is only one week's grace before the second Test at Lord's, but today is a crucial county occasion, the quarter-final of the Benson and Hedges Cup. Edgbaston, however, is anything but a hive of cup fever . . . it rained instead.

The clouds opened shortly after ten o'clock, and the story was much the same as on so many other days this season. Steady, heavy rain, no earthly chance of play, and the boredom lifted only by racing on television. In this case, that wasn't such a bad thing; it was Derby Day, and Barnsley and I roared Remainder Man into third place, delighted for our good friends Reg Hollinshead, the trainer, and jockey Tony Ives.

Instead of the early night that we should probably all have had in preparation for an important cup tie, some of us escorted the very sociable Glamorgan opposition to a pub. Some might call that unprofessional. In football, such behaviour would be greeted with stern cries, fines and suspensions. But the social life remains very much a part of cricket, and I would not wish that changed.

My only criterion for myself and for the young players, in whom I take a lot of pride, is that the following day's performance must never be affected. I leave their private lives to them, but if anyone carries a hangover onto the field and plays as if he would rather bury his head in a tube of Alka-Seltzers, then it is time the high living was cut down to size.

Thursday June 8

Sometimes I think it is beyond Warwickshire to do anything comfortably. We made it through to the semi-finals today, but we walked on water to do so. Midway through the afternoon, I could hardly believe that Flight was getting away with it as frequent delicate bowling changes were forced upon him by our slim resources and the fact that Oliver had conceded 14 runs in his one over. It was a question of 'twist or stick' all afternoon, and somehow we got through, with Andy Lloyd bowling a spell of eleven overs reasonably cheaply; a good effort for one who bowls as infrequently as he does.

We had won the toss and got the ideal start, but a dreadful collapse in mid-morning threatened to send us on our way out. Too many indifferent shots were played, and we were in the mire until Flight's 70 and a fine seventh-wicket stand between Jasper and Rebel, no less, pulled us round. Our eventual 205 was at least something to defend, and after I had removed Alan Jones and Mike Llewellyn a bit hastily, they gave us surprisingly little trouble.

The Cup draw has been kind to us again. We must go to Derby, who went much against the form book in beating Middlesex today. I feel we still have higher hopes against them than either of the other semi-finalists, Kent and Somerset.

Even after defeat, Glamorgan were sociable to the last. They all stayed the night and became pleasantly merry with the rest of us. There are a lot of great guys in the Glamorgan team, and sharing the good times with them makes all the rigours of the circuit worthwhile.

Friday June 9

One of the things a county cricketer learns very early in life is never to mock or moan about benefit games. If you are good enough and loyal enough, your turn will come. I have to confess, however, that there have been seasons when I seem to have done little else but race around the country playing in bun-fights. When they become that frequent, I usually succeed in turning them into an unhappy chore.

This year, with no beneficiary at Warwickshire, things have been easier, and it was no effort at all to play for Mike Brearley at King's Langley, a small town in Hertfordshire ... at least, it shouldn't have been any effort. As things turned out, the whole day narrowly avoided complete chaos.

A phone call from the match organizer woke me up, checking that I was sound in mind and body for the occasion. Only then did it strike me that I was in a mess. My sponsored car had been taken back yesterday, and for transport to Hertfordshire I was, in a word, stuffed.

Scagg was soon on the phone himself, mixing a bit of England team talk with a bit of persuasion, and when I finally got my head together enough, I was prepared to make the trip by train. Phone calls then flashed between King's Langley and Birmingham for an hour or two, exchanging various travel plans, before I arrived at the only sensible conclusion and borrowed one of the Warwickshire Fiats from Geoff Humpage.

It was the regular benefit game routine, signing about two thousand autographs and going through the motions for a few overs, but there was a good turnout on a fine evening, and I was pleasantly impressed by the standard of young ladies around the greenery.

I did the hike back to Birmingham in ninety minutes and settled down to watch a film on the Manson 'Family' which I was keen to see, having read the book in hospital three years ago. I missed it, though – fatigue took over and I tottered up to bed at eleven o'clock.

Saturday June 10

Bit of a confrontation today. Yours truly, representing Warwickshire, against the Black Diamond, alias Wayne Daniel, representing Middlesex. It added up to a frenzied day of cricket at Edgbaston, with Rebel and myself rushing Middlesex out for 155 before the Diamond got his revenge. Our batsmen clearly were unhappy against Daniel, and we were a pitiful 30 for 5 until Abbers and Rebel led a recovery.

That was all blood and thunder stuff, and no doubt great to watch for the few people there; what a tragedy that on a Saturday in June, with the county champions playing, a ground like Edgbaston is almost empty. I find it quite soul-destroying.

Sunday June 11

The decorator was knocking on the door at 7.30 a.m., which shook off the Sunday morning dust, and I was able to make an early start to Stafford to visit a friend.

Chased back to Birmingham for the early Sunday lunch at the ground and the almost stereotyped John Player League story – not enough runs from the batters and not enough control from the bowlers. Our fifth defeat in five games surprised nobody.

Anyone strolling into the sponsors' room after the game would have been treated to the unusual sight of me with a soft drink in my hand. Socially, the past few days seem to have been hectic, and with the next Test only a matter of days distant I felt it was a sensible idea to give alcohol a complete rest.

The evening passed pleasantly. I had a curry with Mike

Brearley at a fine Indian restaurant called The Maharajah, and our conversation is already looking ahead to Australia this winter, and players who might challenge for places. We both agreed that John Lever must go, and Wayne Larkins won a good mention in the young batsmen stakes.

Monday June 12
I have never bowled better in my life. That was the opinion of Mike Brearley and myself after I had taken 5 for 38 to bowl Middlesex out a second time and set us up for a precious victory.

There is a fine borderline between success and failure for fast bowlers; days when the harder you try, the worse you bowl, and others when everything functions so smoothly that the job seems easy. This was one of the latter occasions. I bowled very fast indeed to a seven-two field (seven fielders on the off side and only two on the leg), and seemed able to dictate my line and length far better than ever before. Naturally, I was delighted, even elated, especially as our openers put on 70 without being parted before the close. I celebrated in style with orange juice and soda water at the White Swan.

Tuesday June 13
Wayne Daniel caused some jitters among our batsmen before victory was achieved. He is a formidable pace bowler, but I'm happy to say I believe I bowled better than he did over the course of this match.

The game finished around lunchtime and I was presented with a £200 man-of-the-match award by the sponsors, Bristol Street Motors.

It was pleasant and useful to have an afternoon at home, organizing some double-glazing and taking delivery of a new sponsored car, this time a Granada.

Wednesday June 14

After dropping Ollie and Jasper at Northampton for their county game, I headed for London, where the first stop was the Chelsea studio of an artist named Theo Ramos. I had met him once before and agreed that he should paint my portrait. I also found him a fascinating guy, and posing for him filled in an interesting hour and helped take my mind off the Test match ahead.

Then it was on to Lord's for nets, and my first view this season inside that sacred pavilion. The ground authorities are very strict here; unless you are an MCC or Middlesex member, and you are wearing a jacket and tie, you are not allowed into the pavilion. Women are banned in any case.

There are many stories of frustrated players not being recognized by the gateman at the Grace Gates entrance and being stranded out in St John's Wood Road until someone has been summoned to assure the intransigent guy on the gate that the gentleman outside is who he says he is. Today there were no such diversions. Nothing changes inside the pavilion. It smells of wood polish, blended with that slightly musty aroma that can set the guts churning before a big occasion.

The dressing room, normally used by Middlesex, is hardly what one would expect at cricket's headquarters. Inside the door, which has a slightly cracked frosted glass panel, the room spreads away to the right. The floor is boarded and tiled, somewhat inelegantly, and there is a table in the middle of the room where bats and autograph books will be piled, ready for signing, throughout the game. The seats are a motley collection of old sofas and armchairs, some split and spewing stuffing, and one or two rickety, upright wooden chairs. On the far side of the room are some wash basins and a mirror. The room is on the second floor of the pavilion, and leads out onto a tiny balcony, with two benches where players and selectors sit to look out on the cricket.

1. Warwickshire County Cricket Club team, 1978. Back row, left to right: Alvin Kallicharran, Eddie Hemmings, Steve Perryman, Philip Oliver, Steve Rouse, David Smith, Chris Clifford and Geoff Humpage. Seated, left to right: Neal Abberley, Bob Willis (vice-captain), John Whitehouse (captain), David Brown and Dennis Amiss

2. Jogging to keep fit at the county ground

3. The England team before the Edgbaston Test v. Pakistan. Back row, left to right: Clive Radley, Geoff Miller, Ian Botham, Mike Hendrick, Phil Edmonds, David Gower, Harry Wood. Seated, left to right: Graham Roope, Bob Willis (vice-captain), Mike Brearley (captain), Chris Old, Bob Taylor

4. Shot from the top of the pavilion, a panoramic view of Lord's as I bowl during the second Test against Pakistan

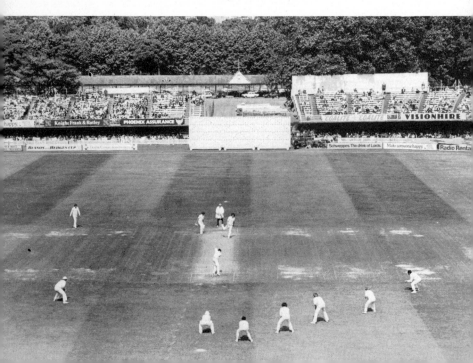

5. It may look daft but it's an excellent way of tuning up. Bernard Thomas (second left) supervises early-morning stretches before the first Test of the summer, at Edgbaston

6. Mike Brearley (left) looks on as Bernard Thomas takes my weight on his shoulder – an exercise that had the cameramen flocking around at Edgbaston. Rather like Little and Large, isn't it?

7. Wayne Daniel, the 'Black Diamond', in action for Middlesex against Warwickshire at Edgbaston, 12 June 1978

8. Iqbal suffers at my hands again, this time less painfully, as his off-stump goes for a walk during the second Test, England v. Pakistan. Notice I was again bowling round the wicket, not to bounce him, but to get a different angle against the left-hander

9. The moment of triumph that any bowler relishes. Umpire Ken Palmer's index finger is on its way to pronounce the lbw sentence on Mohsin Khan early in the weather-ruined third Test at Leeds. Bob Taylor, Mike Brearley and Graham Roope acclaim the wicket in their individual styles

10. Stern determination as I enter my delivery stride at Leeds. Sadiq Mohammad is the non-striker

11. Sleeves rolled high and Warwickshire sweater still on, this is the sight of me that a New Zealander had during the county's tour match at Edgbaston

12. Reflecting on the day's play at Edgbaston while resting my weary legs and feet in my corner of the dressing room

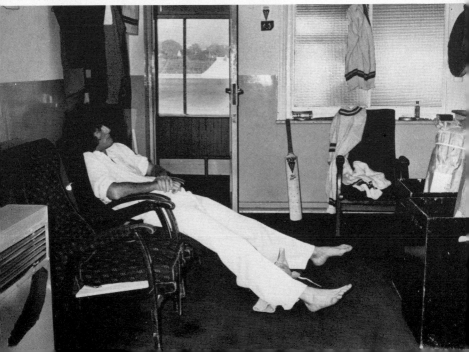

13. Graham Gooch in action during his innings of 94 for England v. New Zealand during the Prudential Trophy match, 15 July 1978

None of this is luxury, but it is reasonably comfortable, and Lord's has much more to offer. The best atmosphere, the best crowds, the best lunches. Unfortunately, no longer the best wickets: some this season have resembled minefields.

The nets today were unsuitable for my needs, so I bowled only two balls, then did some fielding practice, before looking at the wicket. It was a quiet practice session, as we had all been through a busy fortnight.

Bernard Thomas's brand new Rolls-Royce transported me to the team hotel, which on this occasion is the Charing Cross, situated directly above the main-line station. Seems an odd place for a team seeking quiet to stay, with the station noises filtering up into the bedrooms at all hours.

The team dinner was conducted in a relaxed atmosphere, with everyone no doubt more confident about this series after the victory at Edgbaston inside four days. Bouncers were mentioned, and Mike reported that in the wake of Qasim's injury against me at Edgbaston, it is now in the hands of the captains to decide who is capable of receiving bouncers, and how many. I hope it is sensibly sorted out.

We hear that Sarfraz, who bowled for only one session in the first Test before retiring with a strained side, is not fit enough to play. This must be a huge blow to the Pakistanis, for it is difficult to envisage any of the bowlers that remain causing any great devastation.

In our regular chat through the opposition batsmen, we decided that all except Mudassar and Sadiq, the openers, are the sort of players whose freedom of stroke gives the bowlers a chance. We shall see.

Thursday June 15
The World Cup at least gave us an outlet for nervous chatter over breakfast, although I don't think many of us are wildly

interested. The Charing Cross has laid on a private breakfast room for the team, so we can relax without the constant staring and autograph-hunting of other punters in the place.

A disadvantage of this particular hotel, however, is that its car parking accommodation amounts to about half a dozen spaces on the station forecourt. Most of the lads have left their cars at Lord's, and in fear of the West End traffic we decide on an early taxi to the ground. Emerging from the sweeping staircases and relative calm of the hotel, the station at rush-hour time seems another world, and I'm glad to get away. We've overestimated the traffic, however, and get to Lord's at 9.35, which is really too early.

After a look at the wicket, I felt that we ought to bat first, given the choice, and leave out Hendo on the adage that if three seamers can't do the job, four won't.

No sooner had I completed my loosening routine at the nursery end of the ground than rain began to fall. It did not relent for the rest of the day. The ground was full, the perennial first-day feeling at a Lord's Test was growing – and all anyone could do was shelter from the rain. I felt very sorry for all those who had paid for tickets, as there is no such thing as a refund in this game.

The Long Room and the bars in the pavilion are well populated, but I slipped down the side stairs and ran the gauntlet of schoolboys waiting at the door as I headed for the guests' enclosure for a chat and a drink (soft) with Tannoy.

Over lunch, Mike Brearley spoke to me about bouncers. The captains had consulted, he explained, and drawn up a list of five non-recognized batsmen who should at no time receive a bouncer. The list is Hendrick and myself of England, and Liaquat Ali, Sikander Bakht and Iqbal Qasim of Pakistan. I repeated to Mike that I completely disagreed with this system and still felt that everybody should get bouncers, although obviously some discretion must be shown against those less capable. But as all this had come about after the Pakistanis' anger over Qasim's injury at Edgbaston, I suppose it must be accepted.

Mike also said that he thought I should show more sympathy to anyone that I might hit with a short ball. I know he took a lot of stick over the fact that I walked away after hitting Qasim in the face, and he was concerned that I gave the impression of being callously uncaring for my victim. I do care, and Mike accepts that. But I can also see the public's point. My reasons for not getting too involved when I have injured someone is that showing too much sympathy will detract from my concentration. I need to feel right to bowl at my best, and if I stand tending to a bloodied batsman I am not likely to have much fire left in my belly.

After lunch my priority was to acquire some tickets for the Bob Dylan concert at Earl's Court tonight. Anyone who knows me at all realizes that I have a passion for the music of Dylan, and his long-awaited return to this country was something I did not intend to miss.

Before that, though, we all had another appointment to keep . . . with the Queen. We were introduced to the Queen and Prince Philip in the Long Room at five o'clock – it was to have been on the pitch, but the rain was still falling – and I was one of the privileged few invited on into the 'inner sanctum' afterwards for a drink and a chat. I didn't get much of a word with the Queen, but Prince Philip chatted happily about racing, which he follows slightly less fervently than his wife, and said that he was glad that the cricket at Lord's did not clash with Royal Ascot, as he liked to watch both.

From the tea party with the Queen to a concert with Bob Dylan might seem from the sublime to the ridiculous, but I managed to enjoy both enormously, even though the acoustics at Earls Court were poor – a pity, because the man and his band were brilliant.

Friday June 16

I couldn't sleep after about six thirty. I just tossed and turned restlessly, nervously, waiting for the sound of the morning paper flopping onto the room carpet. At least that gave me something to read while I sipped the morning tea, before going down for an early breakfast and setting off for the ground.

The weather had improved dramatically, and we were able to start, forty-five minutes late, at 12.15. Scagg won the toss and I watched the first session with my guests, relieved to see that Tannoy had recovered from his day's drinking on Thursday. Scagg is still out of form, and Rad failed today too. But after these initial setbacks, Graham Gooch and Gower played very well, and it is tremendous to see two such young players looking so confident and attractive in their batting for England.

The entire day was a desperately restless one for me. I never know what to do while we are batting, and I paced interminably before trying to sit down and read some of Mike Brearley's new book on last year's Ashes series. Inside the dressing room, it is all shop talk. Until I started keeping this diary, I had never realized how much of our conversation is dominated by cricket. As I haven't bowled since Monday, I'm feeling lethargic, and the inevitability that I will bowl tomorrow is causing me a little flutter of excitement and a little nervous dread.

Saturday June 17

After less than two full days' cricket, we are in a position to win this game by an innings. We added a few more runs this morning, then ripped through their batting once again. They followed on in the evening session, but they look in a pitiful mess.

As expected, the nerves were at it again this morning, but before leaving for the ground a group of us sat around the breakfast table discussing the curious case of Geoff Boycott. Certainly, he did sustain a thumb injury at Old Trafford. But unless he has now developed arthritis, he must surely have recovered. Most of us are wondering just what he is conjuring up in his complicated head. If he doesn't want to play for England again, he should say so. If he does, I think he should be here with us.

Not that we needed him today. We had, it turned out, made quite enough runs, thanks chiefly to a second successive century from the extraordinary Botham, and the Pakistanis are not really in fighting mood. Their batsmen are, in general, simply not equipped to face top-class bowling on English wickets. Many of them have never played here before, and those who have seem to be suffering from a shortage of form or confidence, or both.

I was pleased with my bowling today and delighted that 'Henry' Edmonds displayed much more control than is sometimes his wont.

Cramp attacked me during the afternoon, and after they had begun their second batting effort it became too painful to carry on. I left the field at 5.30 and soaked in a hot bath before being examined by the doctor, who confirmed that it was nothing more serious. Bernard Thomas suggested it was caused by almost a week of inactivity followed by a lot of bowling today, and said that a day's rest should put it right. I made a mental resolution to resume the early-morning jogging which I have relaxed while there has been so much cricket.

Sunday June 18
I always need this rest day in the middle of a Test match to ease away some of the pent-up tension. Today I also need it to ease away the stiffness of cramp. I walked across Waterloo Bridge after breakfast and took a train to Stoke D'Abernon,

the Surrey village where my folks live. It is a peaceful, sleepy part of the countryside, and that is just what I needed today.

There are times when it is perfect to do absolutely nothing and this was one of them. I lazed in front of the television, dozily watching the World Cup and snatches of the John Player League cricket, but it wasn't until five o'clock that I felt I had really wound down from the Test. Just after eight, I caught a train back to London and went straight to my room for a soak in the bath, a little more football and an early night.

Monday June 19

Although I was awake before seven, for once I had slept soundly. My leg still felt tight, and with the forecast on the room radio predicting a hot, steamy day, I knew I would need all my energy. The thought of a repetition of cramp was worrying.

Reunited with the rest of the side at breakfast, I learned that the press talk was again about bouncers, and again about me. Apparently the Pakistanis took offence at the number of short balls I bowled on Saturday. Most people are also writing off the Pakistanis as a waste of time. Those who are cannot have seen them in their own conditions, and with their own umpires, last winter. It seemed much more difficult for any of our bowlers to get a decision from an umpire out there, and that, allied to the strangeness of the country, gives some idea of the frustrations on what was far from the happiest tour I've been on. I hope we are now reaping our rewards for those nine difficult weeks.

The other subject that the press are, quite naturally, finding it difficult to ignore is that of the captaincy. In terms of results gained, there should be no argument that Mike must be the right man; he still hasn't lost a Test as captain. But his complete loss of form with the bat has brought the vultures crowding round, some of them calling for Boycott.

I know my feelings on the matter, and I believe most of the players feel the same. However much we respect Geoff for his batting and his dedication, we would rather be led by Mike Brearley. Perhaps he took some of the pressure off his head today by leading us to yet another win; although, to be honest, most of us were able to sit back and watch 'Sobers' Botham win it for us.

I had a burst from the pavilion end, which is unusual for me, and rapidly gained in confidence about the cramp-afflicted leg. Mohsin Khan fell to me early on, and the rest surrendered to Botham's magnificent spell. The ball swung for him more than I have ever seen at Lord's — and it did so without any assistance whatever from cloud cover.

It was all over just before lunch, and it had all happened so swiftly that I don't think it sank into anyone's head that we had won the series. Any celebrations were fairly minor, and I found myself in the odd position of not knowing what to do with the next thirty-six hours.

I solved that problem by heading for Earls Court and another evening with Dylan, this time without a ticket. My intention had been to spend some of the win money on lining a tout's pocket, but when I discovered they were asking £40 for a £5 ticket, I rapidly withdrew.

Just as I was despairing of getting in at all, one of the security guards recognized me and I found myself being smuggled through a side door into a place twenty feet from the stage. There are not many occasions when I enjoy being recognized in public, but this was one on which I had no complaints.

5
Wet Weather Miseries

Tuesday June 20

There seems to be little time for commercial work in this crowded cricket schedule, so I was glad to have a day off in which to visit my agent in the West End. Not so long ago, most people in the game would have frowned disapprovingly at any cricketer attempting to supplement his earnings in this way, but the advent of sponsorship and the emergence of more progressive thinkers in the establishment have thankfully swept away many of the archaic ideals.

After a useful day, I drove up to Derby in the early evening, for our Benson and Hedges Cup semi-final tomorrow. A critical occasion for Warwickshire, this, and the rest of the season could be directed by our performance in this game. A victory will ensure that spirit and confidence are maintained for some time to come, but dismissal could have a damaging effect.

Already the news is bad. I was met by Alan Smith ('AC'), our secretary, who reported considerable injury troubles. Kalli has mumps and is already ruled out, but there are severe doubts about Rebel, who is suffering with a knee strain, and Barnsley, who has an injured foot. AC also confided that our negotiations for an overseas player to replace the retired Rohan Kanhai had fallen through. We were back to square one. With that, I went to bed feeling a little depressed.

Wednesday June 21

Just as I don't know a single cricketer who likes the Derby ground, (though it will give universal pleasure to players that money is to be spent on ground improvements, both there and at Northampton) I don't know one who enjoys those dismal days spent trailing on and off the field for bad light. Add the two together, and this must have been one of the worst days in any county cricketer's life. The rain began soon after our arrival on what my pocket diary tells me is the longest day of the year. It seemed like it, too.

We lost the toss and picked Barnsley despite his sore foot. Rebel was left out to rest his knee. Between the showers and the darkest hours, we slotted in five brief sessions, in which Derbyshire made steady and unspectacular progress on the slowest wicket I have seen all season. I have a feeling that this one has been doctored to counteract any pace I might have got out of it, and what is left is absolutely useless to me.

Jasper, Ollie and The Whale all bowled poorly, and I'm afraid we are not in a particularly good position.

Thursday June 22

Woke soon after seven to the sound of the traffic on the wet streets outside my hotel window. There had been more rain during the night and a prompt resumption was out of the question. Rather than return to the boredom of the ground, I spent the morning shopping in Derby, and visited about fifteen shoe shops in search of a pair of $11\frac{1}{2}$ shoes!

The weather improved enough to allow a restart soon after lunch, and we never seriously threatened to challenge Derby's final total of 203. The ball went through the top of the wicket, which is a disgrace in a one-day game, and I was altogether unimpressed with everything about this match. It has also left us with an undoubted problem in lifting the players now that the carrot of a Lord's Cup Final has been snatched away.

Having bought the new Dylan album on my morning's shopping expedition, I cheered myself up before bed with a first spin.

Friday June 23

To start the day in the right mood, I played the Dylan album five times in succession. After that I felt fit to face the world.

Barnsley came round during the morning, feeling very sorry for himself. A bone in his foot is apparently broken and he will be out of the game for some time. That is very bad news, as we are already struggling to get eleven fit and capable players on the field. After cheering him up with a drink and a chat, I settled down to sort through my mail during the afternoon. Much of it followed the bouncer row during the First Test, and a good deal of it was uncomplimentary.

On average, I probably get ten letters a week, the vast majority being simple requests for autographs or photographs. If my picture has appeared in any of the schoolboy comics, it is a safe bet that the cutting will soon be on its way to me for signing, sent by at least a dozen kids. That, I accept, is part of the job, and although it is a chore, I reply to each one uncomplainingly. What does annoy me is when boys at games bring their huge, bulging scrapbooks and ask me to sign about six different pictures. Why they want my autograph more than once is a mystery to me, and those that I have asked never have an answer.

It occurred to me that it would be a good idea to get Tannoy involved in sorting and answering some of my mail. It would not only be a great help to me, but it would give him something to do in his retirement, which up to now seems only to have left him bored.

Saturday June 24

Team selection for the Championship match with Gloucestershire at Edgbaston today was not difficult. Four regular players are out injured, so the rest of the squad were down to play! Poor Barnsley took some ribbing in the dressing room. After his latest injury, someone took to calling him 'Chief Broken Foot'. It's a funny game when you can be that cruel and still all laugh, including the victim.

We batted first and were progressing very nicely until Smithy ran Sacker out; the customary slide followed.

At lunchtime, I went up to keep an appointment at St Andrew's Church in Moseley, where I opened a fête. They were very pleasant people and presented the three of us who went – Ollie and Barnsley were the others – with a bottle of grog.

Back at the ground, I felt oddly jaded. The season is not yet halfway over and there are still four Tests to come, so I must keep myself going. With things not going too well for Warwickshire, it would be all too easy to opt out – not to bother in the county games and just bide my time until the Tests. It has been done before and it will be done again, but I am determined that no one will ever have grounds to accuse me of that.

My efforts with the willow this afternoon raised only six runs before I managed to miss a straight one, and we were bowled out for a disappointing 177, The Whale contributing a gallant 30-odd not out. We were left with half an hour in the field, and I removed Alan Tait in the final over.

Talking of Taity, he brightened the evening for us all. A very amusing man, who trades on his thick Geordie accent, he kept us all rich with laughter during a very pleasant social occasion, wound up with supper at The Towrope for the benefit of those of the Gloucester boys who had not sampled its delights previously.

Sunday June 25

Two hours visiting a friend in hospital in the morning were followed by our seventh successive John Player League defeat, this time at the hands of a Surrey team whose record is almost as impoverished as ours. We have tried almost every imaginable theory on Sundays without success. Now, I fear, the guys' minds are not on the game, and I really can't blame them.

It was World Cup Final night, and I accepted an invitation to attend a showing of it on giant screens at a cabaret evening in the city. The match was enjoyable enough, but the comedian who followed did little else but mock Scotland's performance in Argentina. Nobody laughed much, and as one of the guests was Scotland's captain Bruce Rioch, I thought it was all in pretty bad taste.

Monday June 26

Our prospects in the Championship fixture with Gloucester were further damaged by the news that Steve Perryman had a finger injury and was unable to bowl. The subsequent attack of Willis, Hopkins, Hemmings and Flower was unlikely to frighten anyone, and so it proved. We did reduce them to 102 for five, but between lunch and tea I saw what must have been some of the worst bowling ever in first-class cricket. Two very moderate batsmen, Jim Foat and David Graveney, put on about 200, and it was not until we claimed the second new ball that they were split.

I finished with 7 for 63, but with all three of the other regular seamers missing I am being forced to bowl too many overs in an effort to compensate. After tea I strained a tendon in my right shin, and it remained very painful for the rest of the day.

While I was bowling, I found that a number of the Dylan songs from the new album were racing through my mind. It was a pleasant enough sensation, and certainly didn't bother my concentration at all.

Tuesday June 27

Yesterday's exertions left me feeling very tired, and I was thankful that we didn't have to take the field at any stage. With no possible chance of winning the game, there was no point in trying to set a target, and we concentrated instead on getting some decent batting practice. This was accomplished, as we saw the day through with about 400 for 4 when bad light brought the contest to an early close.

My shin is still sore, and it could be a worry for the Test starting in two days' time. During the day, I had some treatment from Bernard Thomas's assistant Keith Hallam. Keith is blind, and very good-natured, which he needs to be to take some of the pranks that the lads play on him. A favourite example is putting blue cheese in his spotted dick when he eats with us, or covering his dinner with a plate so that cutlery meets crockery as he tries to start his meal. Childish, but good fun, and he sees it that way, giving back plenty of stick himself.

Wednesday June 28

Just before midday, I set off for Leeds and a Test match in which our greatest difficulty could be avoiding the subconscious drop in performance when a series has already been won.

The best nets in the country for batting practice were set

up, as usual, just in front of the pavilion, and we were met by the sight of G. Boycott having a bat against Ray Illingworth, who will next year become his manager at Yorkshire. Fiery still does not consider himself fit enough to come back to Test cricket, and several of us discussed his attitudes later in the day. I don't think anyone in the side claims to understand him and his unwillingness to cooperate as any other individual would. It has been said that Geoff seems to believe he has a God-given right to captain England, and to bear a grudge about the fact that other people don't think similarly.

Nevertheless, I am a great believer in always picking the best side, and whenever he does decide to make himself available again I think he ought to be chosen.

Scagg, meanwhile, is now clearly worried about his batting form, and he had the longest net of anyone this afternoon. I do hope he makes some runs in this Test. It will bring relief to us all.

At the usual team dinner, this time held at the huge and modern Dragonara in the centre of Leeds, an understandable confidence came through from everyone. We all feel that we are a better side than Pakistan, and it would be nice to clean them up for a third time.

Thursday June 29
The weather forecast was for overcast conditions with some rain, but the clouds were high when I came down to breakfast, and the nerves distant enough for me to indulge in a very relaxed chat with Scagg over paintings as decorations for our respective homes. It was in both of our minds to impress upon the lads that we must not take things easily in this Test. There is a potentially tougher series against New Zealand to follow, and we need to keep at a peak in preparation.

Unfortunately, the forecasters were right, and directly after the captains had tossed, a steady, heavy drizzle began which was to last for several hours. One would have thought that with so many days lost to rain this season, I might have formulated some pastime for avoiding restless boredom by now. But I haven't, and after my exercise routine with Bernie, I took the opportunity of studying what the other lads do at times like these.

Scagg left the main dressing room and closetted himself in one of the treatment rooms with a weighty volume called *The Raj Quartet* – four interlinked novels about India at the time of the Raj, by Paul Scott. Mike finds India fascinating, and many were the times that he would slip away from the group to examine some cultural aspect or other during our tour there two winters ago. He is also an avid reader, and tends to choose one major work to last him through the idle moments of a season. Last year it was *Anna Karenina*, and he tells me he just failed to finish it.

Graham Gooch, 'Cyril' Roope, Hendo and 'Guy' are interested in tennis, and although it was also raining at Wimbledon, they were kept entertained by filmed flashbacks of previous matches on television.

When he wasn't watching the tennis, Guy was arguing heatedly with Phil Edmonds. Anyone new to the dressing room might shrink in alarm, fearing he had interrupted one of the world's greatest rows. But these quarrels, generally about some item of world controversy, are an almost daily feature for two guys whose relationship I find very difficult to define.

Philip, with his university education, upper-class breeding and slightly arrogant exterior, has won a new nickname, 'Margaret', as the leader of the opposition. He will argue about anything just for the sake of being different. Guy, although coming from a very different background, is an aggressive, effervescent character who rises to the bait. However fierce their exchanges may become, and however many insults they may cheerfully hurl at each other, they remain close friends both on and off the field.

On the other side of the bright, well aired Leeds dressing room, Chilly was busy with his many friends, organizing benefit functions for next year.

And outside on the balcony, umpires Dickie Bird and Ken Palmer surveyed the bleak scene a little hopelessly. There is a big crowd in the ground, and once again I find myself feeling sorry for every one of them.

Play eventually began at five o'clock, in damp conditions and on a very slow wicket. Pakistan were batting first, and I found rhythm elusive and incentive absent. The wicket did very little to help any of our bowlers, and it was hard to envisage us rolling them over quite so dramatically as we have done in the two previous Tests.

Friday June 30

A resumption of heavy rain at 10.30 this morning condemned us to another boredom fight for much of the day.

It got so bad today that even Scagg joined in when a card school was set up – an unusual sight indeed. Along with Hendo, Dusty, David Gower and Ian Botham, the captain played 'Shoot', which to me, a complete innocent about cards, seemed a good way of losing money quickly.

Scagg remains superficially relaxed, but deep down he must be wondering if he is really a Test-class batsman or not. I think he has also lost some respect for some members of the press, who seem to expect all his felicitudes and welcomings whenever they want to come into the dressing room, and then slate him to death in their columns. He has come around to the view I have long held, that it is far easier not to read the papers at all.

The poor umpires were booed and jeered every time they

even appeared on the balcony. Although I have sympathy with the crowd, they really don't understand the difficulties umpires face, both in deciding when the light is fit enough and when the surrounds are dry enough. For much of today, both were too bad for cricket.

We amplified the crowd's anger by going out at 3.20 and then retreating without bowling a ball because the light was too grim. At four o'clock, however, they did get some cricket, and the final session of the day was played in bright, warm sunshine. Pakistan were progressing quite comfortably until I intervened with two wickets in two balls. I really feel I am fitter, and bowling faster, than at any time in my life. It's a great feeling.

Saturday July 1
Worse and worse. No play at all today, after torrential over-night rain had put the ground under water. The question of adequate covering has now been raised, and there seems no doubt that the covers used here at Headingley are very flimsy, and just don't exist when it comes to properly covering the surrounds and run-ups. Yorkshire have already taken some criticism for this, but to be fair, I don't think it should be their baby. Cornhill Insurance have poured a great deal of money into Test cricket, and it should be down to the Test and County Cricket Board to ensure that the facilities on all their grounds are up to scratch. The umpires have been put under very unfair pressure here, and that should be avoided in future.

Back in the boredom room, the card school operated again, but I found it no more attractive than yesterday. I preferred to stroll about, paying occasional visits to the stand where Tannoy and a few friends were patiently waiting for some play. It was a forlorn hope, and after just five hours' play over

three days, this already seems one of the longest non-events in
cricket history.

Sunday July 2

Many cricketers enjoy an energetic rest day on the golf course,
but I prefer to slip right away from everything, either by
myself or with my folks. As Tannoy is up in Leeds for the
whole game, we had arranged an outing together, driving
across the Dales to a fine old Yorkshire pub, then to a friend's
house for a very good Sunday lunch.

Returned to the hotel in early evening, and shared a quick
drink with Graham Roope, who, as ever, talked non-stop.

Monday July 3

A few minutes before we began our innings today, the selectors took Mike Brearley aside and told him he was to captain
the side for the rest of the summer. It was a sensible and popular choice, and I'm pleased that they had the presence of mind
to put Mike out of his misery before he went out to bat. Not, in
the event, that it made any difference at all. He was out for
nought in the first over, and the Yorkshire crowd which had
given him an unwelcoming reception when he walked out
gave him an even rougher time on his way back.

Not unnaturally, the people up here want their own man
Boycott in the side, and as captain. At least I imagined that
was how they all felt until I chatted to a few this afternoon and
was told in no uncertain terms that a fair proportion of Yorkshire followers would be only too pleased if Fiery went to
another county – as has been rumoured.

We had bowled Pakistan out very rapidly this morning at
the start of another overcast, dismal day. My feet slid around
on the wet surface, but Guy and Chilly bowled so well that I

was hardly needed. Pakistan have a fearfully long tail and we exposed it once again.

Our own batting was unconvincing. Apart from Mike, who managed to remain philosophical despite his obvious depression, too many poor shots were played by batsmen who seem unable to accept that we are playing a five-day game and that, consequently, there is no need to hurry. In this case, of course, so much of the Test had been lost already that a result was almost completely out of the question. Perhaps I am too critical of batsmen when I see wickets tumbling; I certainly fret more than I would like to.

The hospitality of Cornhill, though much appreciated, was not very inviting tonight, as the tent seemed rather overfull of people who had quite blatantly spent the day on the booze. I escaped quickly and enjoyed a good meal at the Dragonara with some of the lads. We actually managed to keep the conversation away from cricket for most of the evening, eventually getting round to discussing who we most hated on television. My own vote went to Esther Rantzen, the toothy lady who has made herself such a star in That's Life, but the rest of the poll was scooped by quizmasters Nicholas Parsons and Hughie Green.

Tuesday July 4
A Test that has been completely and successfully mocked by the weather tapered away into nothing and was abandoned just after four o'clock.

Play was delayed again, and when we started Sarfraz picked up some cheap wickets and almost bowled us out. It meant very little, however, and I can't say that I was sorry to see the back of Leeds and set off on the cripplingly long journey to Taunton, for tomorrow's Gillette Cup tie.

6
Crisis Point

Wednesday July 5

Placed indifferently midway in the Championship and cat-astrophically close to the bottom of the John Player League, Warwickshire had only the Gillette Cup left to occupy their dreams. Now, after the most unbelievable one-day match I have ever played in, we don't even have that. Somerset and Warwickshire scored almost 600 runs between them on a day stunningly dominated by batsmen. But even now, hours after the final ball was bowled, I find it difficult to accept that we lost.

It always had the makings of an entertaining game, and the thought of pitting my bowling against the formidable Viv Richards, not to mention Guy the Gorilla, had persuaded me into bed soon after ten o'clock when I arrived at Taunton's County Hotel from Leeds last night. Before long, however, Brown, Lloyd and Oliver bounced breezily into my room to relate tales from their day at Warwick races, a very social event although it emptied their pockets.

This morning, I felt below my best, the lack of decent sleep in recent days giving me an unwanted sense of detachment from events. Perhaps this contributed to my muddled think-ing when I inspected the wicket before play began and arrived at the priceless conclusion that this would be a low-scoring game. I haven't been allowed to forget that quote.

Our batsmen did their job blamelessly, compiling a score of 292 that had previously never been exceeded by a team batting second in a Gillette tie. Understandably, we took the field feeling confident.

It was Richards, almost inevitably, who savaged our pride and our hopes with a match-winning century. There can be no better batsman in the world than this fellow, and he turned on his full, irresistible power as if he was flicking a switch. I will always believe that I had him out, caught behind, when he had scored 60. But he didn't walk, and the umpire gave him 'not out'. With that escape, I believe the game swung Somerset's way. As the battering continued, our fielding became ragged, and by the end we looked a poor and purposeless side. But then, against Richards in this form, not many teams could have looked good.

The dreadful disappointment of a defeat when one had almost expected victory was mirrored in our dressing room and in the bar after the game. Joking was out; the customary ribald humour in desperately short supply. And, although several of the lads did stay for a drink, it was a subdued occasion.

Rather than attempt the long trek back to Birmingham tonight, I had arranged to stay with Ian Botham and his wife at their 'second home' in Weston-super-Mare. Together, victor and vanquished re-lived an extraordinary day's cricket over the evening meal.

Friday July 7
To many people who watch the game, I suppose I have always been 'that one with the long, curly hair'. My locks have become something of a trademark over the years, especially as I grew them fashionably longer at about the time that I

overcame my fitness problems of 1976 and got back into the England side.

The fact is, I like my hair long, and although it has excited one or two bitter criticisms from traditionalists, it has certainly never adversely affected my cricket. Today, though, I decided that enough was enough, and duly paid my money for the annual operation. Quite a severe cut, actually, and there was no way I would escape the mickey-taking in the dressing room when I reported to the ground at midday.

There are a number of very humorous individuals in the Warwickshire dressing-room, but in attempting to describe them I've found that cricket humour does not translate well from the spoken to the written word. Much of it can be vulgar, though not obscenely so, and almost all of the laughs are gained at the expense of another member of the team. It is sharp, instant wit that loses everything in repetition. Today I was a heaven-sent target for the jokers, with most of my curls left on the barber's floor.

Saturday July 8
The defeat at Taunton has had a worse effect on the side than I feared. With nothing tangible left to play for, some of the on-field spirit is visibly draining away, and today's performance against Yorkshire at Bradford left me depressed about the team's future. Four catches were dropped. John Hampshire went on to reap a century and put Yorkshire in a very good position.

I spent the evening dining with Barnsley and jockey Tony Ives, a good and long-standing friend, but although the occasion and the company were pleasant, I found it hard to take my mind off the problems that now confront the county team.

Sunday July 9
Less than a week after the end of that seemingly interminable
Test, I found myself back at Leeds. This time the weather was
better, but our fortunes at John Player League cricket don't
improve. We suffered yet another defeat and the day was only
lightened by renewing acquaintances with some of the very
charming staff at the Headingley ground.

Monday July 10
Back at Bradford, we were bowled out soon after lunch for 85;
Yorkshire employed the afternoon for some swift runs and set
us 328 just before the close. If that wasn't a gloomy day for
Warwickshire, I don't know what is.

I was reminded of the huge contrasts affecting my season as
I split my time between a buoyant England side that can currently do no wrong, and a Warwickshire team in a tricky
period. It is an odd situation, calling almost for a dual personality . . . but I think far too much of Warwickshire to give up
and go through the motions as they struggle.

However, I genuinely feel that I need a rest, and wouldn't at
all mind missing the county's match with the New Zealand
tourists which starts on Wednesday.

Tuesday July 11
We made a better fist of the run chase against Yorkshire than
had seemed likely. Just after tea, in fact, there was a chance
that we might even pull off a surprise win, which might have
done something to boost morale and ease the current tension.
But Chilly returned to the attack, bowling magnificently, and
Yorkshire completed a victory that I must say they deserved.

Unfortunately, my hopes of a rest over the next three days
came to nothing. After a number of phone calls, involving the

coach, the captain and myself, it was decided that it would be a slight on the tourists if we fielded an under-strength side. I didn't think my request was unreasonable, my point being that I have so far had a very busy season bowling for England and Warwickhire and that I deserved a break. It would also have given us a chance to field David Hopkins, our promising young inswing bowler.

But despite these problems, Bradford has been an enjoyable trip. Yorkshiremen in general may not be my favourite folk, but I found the people here very friendly. The girls behind the bar and the tea ladies were charming, and the Yorkshire masseur – a big, bluff chap they call 'The Rubber' in these parts – kept us in stitches throughout the day with his stories. A great character, and it was a good job he was here.

Wednesday July 12

Still hung over from yesterday's defeat, our batting against the touring New Zealanders was again inconclusive, and having been looking forward to a day with my feet up, I had to strap my pads on in mid-afternoon. Shortly afterwards, when we took the field, I didn't have the usual amount of aggression and determination in my opening spell with the new ball. John Wright and Geoff Howarth, the New Zealand openers, were relieved and untroubled.

I spent the evening chatting to John Parker, Mark Burgess, Bev Congdon and my old mate 'Kiwi' Howarth, all of whom are very conversant with the English county scene. Over several lagers, we all agreed that tourists' matches against the counties could somehow be made more competitive. It is the trend in some counties to rest both strike bowlers and front-line batsmen in these games, the consequences being that the touring side get little significant practice and the result means little to the county.

These four guys in particular among the current New Zealand side appreciate the problems associated with a long season and the difficulty in motivating oneself for games such as this.

Thursday July 13
The Kiwis are a very friendly bunch and I arranged a small party for them at my house tonight. Most of them came and were appreciative. It was an enjoyable evening, but I probably spent too much of it talking over our team's problems with Alan Oakman rather than entertaining my guests.

The cricketing day had belonged to Bev Congdon and John Parker, who relished batting against our attack and each scored centuries. We seem to be doing England no favours at all by playing the New Zealanders into form.

I feel very sorry for Chris Clifford, who is making his Warwickshire debut. He has come into the side at a time when few players are doing themselves justice. It must be slightly discouraging for him, just as our present form is disturbing for us all. Although we are not especially well equipped on the playing side, I am sure the potential is there. It has to be accepted that we are in a period of change and still rebuilding from the heady days of 1972, when all but one of the first eleven were Test players.

I don't expect an overnight transition to such triumphs, but I believe that, in David Smith, Phil Oliver and Andy Lloyd we have the young talent to mix in with the experience. In short, we ought to be achieving much more than we are.

Friday July 14
Warwickshire cricket reached an all-time low this morning as

we contrived to lose seven wickets in forty minutes, and so a match in which I found it difficult to feel totally involved finished in humiliating defeat by twenty to twelve. If my bowling wasn't all it should have been, my batting was worse, culminating this morning in a dreadful cross-batted swish. Willis bowled Hadlee 0 . . .

The time to talk things over being considerably extended by our hasty submission, the first priority was a selection meeting with the captain and the coach. I again repeated that Lloyd, Smith and Oliver should play in the next game, coupling this with a push for Clifford, who I now believe is the best of the current spinners. Flight, however, wanted to keep the same side together until after the four days at Colchester, because a week's break follows in which to reassess. This, being undoubted logic, was agreed upon.

At three o'clock, I left Edgbaston with Bernard Thomas, this time in a borrowed Rolls-Royce. Our destination, for the third time in a fortnight, was Yorkshire. This time, Scarborough, for the first of the Prudential one-day internationals against New Zealand. But, on the journey up, conversation drifted inevitably towards Warwickshire's worries. I felt that the club must be firmer in its judgement of players. They must find out if the professionals on their staff will make the grade. If they fail, they must be told they would be better off doing something else. It may sound an uncompromising attitude, but I see it as the only way to build a capable playing staff, and it is also entirely fair, in the long run, to the individual.

Turning off from county matters and concentrating once again on England was not an easy mental process, but a pleasant dinner relaxed me and attuned my mind to the new challenge ahead. I was in bed quite early and had actually got off to sleep when the phone rang just before midnight. It was a Yorkshire member I had neither met nor heard of, asking if I

would meet his daughter tomorrow. I don't recall the words of
my reply, but I'm certain they weren't encouraging. It was
three o'clock before I managed to sleep again.

7
Hypnosis

Saturday July 15

New Zealand, I had always thought, should provide us with far sterner opposition than Pakistan, if for no other reason than that their climate and playing conditions are so much more similar to ours than are the dust-tracks of Karachi and Lahore. We beat them today, in the opening joust of the contest, and beat them comfortably, but they still acquitted themselves capably enough to leave my first opinion unaltered.

Scarborough on a July Saturday can be one of the delights of a cricket season, and although the weather at first was overcast the atmosphere this morning was warm and friendly, with a big holiday crowd filling this seaside ground. It is a ground famous for its annual end-of-season cricket festival, but bringing a one-day international here was a brave and successful move.

With a lot of cloud around, the toss could have been crucial, and we would certainly have put them in if we had won it. In the event, Mark Burgess called correctly, and asked us to bat first. All the problems we had anticipated against the swinging ball were overcome by Graham Gooch. Opening with Mike Brearley, Goochy batted quite beautifully for 94 and richly deserved those missing six runs. After getting ourselves into the ideal position, however, we fell away over the last ten overs and had to settle for 206; reasonable but far from invincible.

The strength and consistency of our bowling was once again too much for an opposing team to cope with. New Zealand scored steadily, but were never in a position to challenge for victory, and we finished good winners.

The one blot on my horizon was that John Wright, the Derbyshire left-hander, again played me very well and scored quite heavily. In New Zealand last winter, he was the batsman who always held us up, and always played particularly well against me. It is worrying for any bowler when an opposing team possesses someone you cannot disturb or dislodge, and I know I am going to need to work especially hard against Wright in the coming series.

John Lever and Derek Randall, two great characters, were back in the England side today, and the spirit, already high, profited accordingly. Derek is known to all as 'Arkle' for his galloping running action, and as usual he flitted around the dressing room like a bumble bee, unable to settle and living on his nerves. A batsman of considerable talent, Arkle probably suffers more problems from his mind than his technique.

Despite yet another good performance as captain, Scagg came in for some more verbal hammer from the Yorkshire crowd, and it is now clearly getting through to him. Understandably, I think he is wondering just what he must do to win their support.

The New Zealanders, meanwhile, didn't seem too deflated after their defeat, judging by the fact that they were still conducting a hearty sing-song at their hotel in the early hours of Sunday morning.

Sunday July 16
Slept late after the extravagances of last night, and dismissed

breakfast as a bad plan. Set off in mid-morning with JK and Bernard for the drive over the Yorkshire moors to the M62 and on to Manchester for tomorrow's second international.

Having indulged in a long and sociable lunch at a pub known to JK and me, it was after three o'clock when we arrived at the leafy country-house scene of the Mottram Hall Hotel, our base for the next game. I caught up on some sleep, then chatted to Scagg about the make-up of the team, both for tomorrow and, more important, for the first Test against the New Zealanders.

Geoff Boycott's name was inevitably mentioned, and I agreed with Scagg that he must, if available, come back into the Test side. That would leave Graham Roope's place in severe doubt, which is unfortunate for a man who has never really let us down, despite my personal feelings that he is just that vital level below Test standard.

The other problem that occurred to us was that Chris Old, who had pulled out of the Prudentials with a shoulder injury, may not be fit in time for the Test. In that event, his position would fall either to Mike Hendrick or John Lever, and although JK bowled exceptionally well at Scarborough, Hendo's three-match sentence as twelfth man so far this season would probably win him the vote.

Before going out to eat, I listened to the John Player League results and felt both surprised and delighted that Warwickshire had beaten Essex at Colchester. It may not have been the greatest week of my association with the county, but my loyalty to the club remains as strong as ever. I hate to see them doing badly, and I just hope now that this victory may have given the morale a lift.

Monday July 17
Doubts about the potential of this New Zealand side are, after

all, creeping into everyone's thoughts after their almost em-
barrassingly heavy defeat at Old Trafford today. But for a
carnival innings of 60 hit-and-hope runs by Lance Cairns, our
margin of victory would have been immense, and despite the
fundamental differences between Test and one-day combat, it
could have done the Kiwis' confidence no good whatever.

We do seem to have a great deal of expert limited-overs
players in this country now, but perhaps none better than
Clive Radley, whose century today was typically scamper-
and-smash. He is terrifically fast between the wickets, turning
ones into twos and twos into threes, and his attacking shots,
though anything but textbook orthodox, are superbly effective.

Our total was formidable and New Zealand never got into a
chase at all, which was a great relief after the problems we had
been through in sorting out who was going to play.

We had all been up and on the road early, as the one disadvantage of the otherwise ideal Mottram Hall is that it leaves
us with a sixteen-mile drive to the ground, some of it on
heavily congested roads. When we got there, Scagg and I had
our usual look at the wicket, and Scagg decided that it would
turn and immediately revised his initial plan to leave out
Miller and Roope. Dusty was restored to the side and we were
suddenly overloaded with bowlers.

I volunteered to stand down, so that the selectors could
study and compare the form and fortunes of Hendo and JK,
but the decision was eventually taken out of our hands when
Hendo announced that he had a slight niggle in his back. We
won the toss, and Rad's century won the match, scooping our
fourth victory in four Prudential matches this season.

Our elation was cooled a little by the discovery that the
baths and showers were cold – a problem that we had encoun-
tered at Taunton two weeks earlier – and nobody felt inclined
to linger and freeze. The bar seemed far more inviting, and it

was there that I aired one of my pet grouses to the Test and County Cricket Board's promotions chief, Peter Lush.

I based my argument on the day's official attendance and receipts. More than 13,000 people had watched the game, yet only 6000 had paid to come in. The rest, as Lancashire members, were allowed in free. Surely, I suggested to Peter Lush, county members have enough privileges for the relative pittance they pay annually, without giving them free tickets for international games as well. I believe that, with the admission charges for the general public increasing almost yearly, it is time everyone had to pay for these games. I then rested my case and drove home to Birmingham with Bernard, fatigue overtaking me once again.

Tuesday July 18

Nerves are very much a part of my life. So too is insomnia. In attempts to ease both problems, I accepted the help of an Australian doctor of hypnotherapy, Arthur Jackson. The results have been remarkable.

I first met Arthur in Sydney during the 1974–75 tour. We had just lost the fourth Test – and with it, The Ashes – and while the main body of the squad flew off to play in Tasmania, three of us were left in Sydney to rest. Just before the team departed, manager Alec Bedser had received a telephone call from Dr Jackson, inviting any of the team to a barbecue he was organizing. As things turned out I went alone, and I have every reason to be thankful for accepting that invitation.

Arthur and I got on quite well from the start. He was interested in cricket and, although I was slightly sceptical of the way he earned his living, I at least found it interesting to discuss hypnosis. Over the next two years, he and I corresponded occasionally, but I didn't meet him again until March 1977 – at another barbecue, already well-chronicled for the fact that

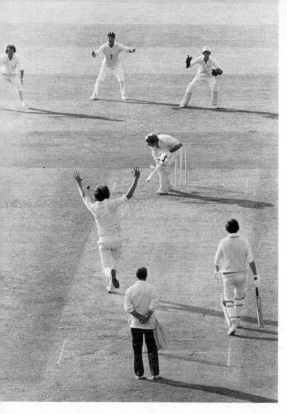

14. I don't enjoy bowling at The Oval, but this was a happy moment. New Zealand's captain Mark Burgess is lbw to me playing half-forward during the first Test of the series

15. A prized and premeditated wicket. Geoff Howarth chased a widish half-volley and dragged it into his stumps at The Oval. Scagg is delighted, Chat looks staggered and I look as though I'm about to perform a handspring

16. The Oval again, and Burgess gets well beneath another Willis bouncer

17. A boundary off Steve Boock gives David Gower his maiden Test century during the Oval Test

18. Young Warwickshire opening batsman David Smith scored a fine 132 not out for Warwickshire v. Sussex at Edgbaston, August 1978

19. Two fast bowlers in actio
Richard Hadlee and myself

1978 season: New Zealand's

20. *Left* Allowing himself the luxury of a smile of satisfaction, Geoff Boycott wipes the sweat from his brow and neck after scoring a century for England v. New Zealand at Trent Bridge

21. *Right* A square drive to the boundary for Mike Brearley during his 50 in the Trent Bridge Test

22. General delight from the England team as Bob Anderson, the New Zealand opening batsman, is run out at Trent Bridge by a direct throw on to the stumps

23. I don't get a lot of opportunity with the bat, but I'm rather proud of the fact that more than half of my Test innings have been undefeated. I don't look as if I'm enjoying the experience too much on this occasion, during the third Test against New Zealand at Lord's, however

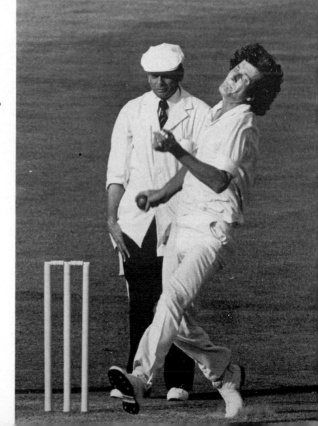

24. Umpire Dickie Bird checking me for overstepping at Lord's, where he also surprised me with a warning for over-use of the bouncer

it was there that Tony Greig dropped the first hints of Kerry Packer's bombshell.

At that time I was nervy, overwrought and extremely tired. It was the end of a very long tour, including five Tests in India, a shrivellingly hot fortnight in Sri Lanka, and of course the Centenary Test in Melbourne.

I was only too well aware that I had bowled dreadfully in the second innings of the Centenary game. Fatigue had got the better of me, and my bowling suffered. I mentioned this to Arthur and he suggested that I should allow him to hypnotize me. At first I had strong doubts – the usual layman's fears about the mysteries of hypnosis and what happens when you are 'under' – but I agreed, and attended Arthur's surgery along with England team-mate Graham Barlow.

It was an extraordinary experience. I lay down on his sofa feeling as if the cares of the cricket world were supported only by my shoulders. I got up an hour later feeling totally refreshed and alive – even relatively carefree. The success of this single session prompted us to experiment. Arthur made a cassette recording of his own voice, talking through the hypnosis process, and I have kept it ever since. It isn't quite so effective as the 'live' sound of his voice, but it has changed my life in that I know relief from tension is always available.

With me, the shortage of sleep is as much a psychological barrier as a physical fault. I have probably trained my mind to the belief that I need eight or nine hours of sleep each night. In fact, I am sure I can happily survive on much less, but the subconscious wins, and when I fall below that stipulated number of hours I feel I ought to be tired. Excessive fatigue then takes over and I find it difficult to sleep at all.

The greatest problems occur on my first night in a strange room – and in this job, that adds up to a lot of nights. To help me, the Test and County Cricket Board always arrange that I should have a double bed whenever I am playing for England, as I find a single bed almost impossible.

Hypnosis has not completely overcome these problems, of course. But it has been an enormous help. During a disturbed night, or if I wake unnecessarily early with worries whizzing around my head, I will often switch on the tape recorder to put myself back in a relaxed state.

The tape lasts about thirty minutes and begins in the time-honoured fashion of hypnosis with instructions to sit or lie down, then slowly relax each part of my body in turn. From my toes up to my face, Arthur talks me through the process, urging me to concentrate on letting go. He then tells me to imagine I'm at the top of a staircase, perhaps leading down to a piece of rural paradise. There are fifty steps, he says, and I must count down from fifty to nothing as I imagine myself descending into this idyllic situation.

I feel quite deeply entranced by this time, but he takes me deeper still. Counting from one up to ten, he asks me to open my eyes at five, then feel the overpowering urge to slowly close them again. To make this a success, you have to want these things to happen – and when you do, the sensation is of being at peace with everything.

I am now totally relaxed, physically and mentally, and the second stage of the process begins . . . confidence building. My biggest problem in cricket used to be that I thought I was in the England team by default – I would not accept that I was better than the rest. So while I am under the hypnosis, Arthur tells me that I will be positive in everything I do and say; that negative feelings will disappear. He tells me that I will show great enthusiasm and interest in everything and that I will never feel any sense of boredom while I am playing cricket. Test cricket is all about the ability to retain one's concentration over a long period, and this is another thing he verbally instils in me.

I am only brought out of this state by a final count from one to ten. On the count of five, I am told, my eyes will open again and I will gradually return to the normal world.

Someone new to hypnosis would probably laugh at this description. Three years ago, I might have laughed with them. But in the condition I felt at six o'clock this morning, my whole head buzzing after a dreadfully fitful night, I was very thankful that I took the trouble to learn from Arthur Jackson. Having listened to the tape, I slept pleasantly for another two hours before getting up and reporting to Edgbaston. I felt well again, more relaxed – just as I have done on the half dozen previous occasions this season when I have had to turn to the tape for comfort and relief.

The cricket talk didn't hold me today, though, so I didn't linger at the ground after lunch. Instead, I tended my garden . . .

Wednesday July 19
Just to emphasize how tired I am, I managed to sleep through a lazy afternoon today and, as one who finds sleeping in daylight hours almost impossible, that is worthy of note.

Thursday July 20
The importance that is being placed in this winter's Ashes series can be gauged by the fact that I spent most of today bowling, catching and posing for a promotional film designed entirely to boost our games and detract from those played under the Packer banner. Some of it was straightforward, if rather exhausting, but I found the simulated appeals, and the supposed joy after taking a wicket, rather unnatural to perform against an invisible batsman and with no spectators in the ground but for a few curious Warwickshire players.

Friday July 21

For some weeks past, I had this date pencilled in for a party, so long as we were not required to play in the Benson and Hedges Cup Final on the following day. As that pleasure had escaped us, the binge was on. As always on these occasions, the preparations took longer than the actual event. I was back home from practice by 12.30, and after refuelling Barnsley, who had come round for a chat and a drink, I spent the afternoon and early evening getting everything ready. At 7.30, I slumped into an armchair, surveyed the tidy yet deserted scene, and tried to conjure up a vision of how it might look in about four or five hours' time, crammed full of pulsating bodies. I shuddered.

The night was fine, fortunately, and most of the revellers opted for the back garden, fighting off the gnats. The Warwickshire team was there in force, of course. Various other friends made up a very healthy number, judging by the fact that twenty-two gallons of beer were consumed, and I didn't get to bed until after five o'clock.

Saturday July 22

Most of you will know what comes next, I'm sure. Anyone who has ever hosted a party recognizes the dread of getting up the morning after, your head telling you that you are in anything but mid-season form, and facing the debris of a disaster movie in your own front room.

I can't say I was around at the crack of dawn, because I'd only just got to bed then, but it was at least still morning when I plucked up courage to face the clearing-up operation and found to my relief that it was not quite so devastating as I had imagined. True, there were a few glasses in the hedgerows, and the sight of ham floating in mushy strawberries did nothing for the delicate state of my stomach. But Jim Cumbes and wife Liz came round to help out, and by lunchtime the worst was past.

The rest of the day passed in relaxed fashion, watching the Benson and Hedges Final and feeling very sorry for my pals in the outplayed Derbyshire side.

Sunday July 23
The rain woke me up and I wasn't especially sorry to hear it. I was of the impression that there were more important issues to be resolved at Edgbaston today than the destination of four Sunday League points.

Alan Oakman phoned me to say that the customary Sunday morning nets were cancelled due to the weather, but I reported to the ground at the regular time and took to the Colts Ground for some running. It is six days since I played last, and sixteen laps at least shook off the cobwebs.

Any chance of play today was disappearing rapidly, and what was to be a critical selection meeting began soon after lunch. The team to play a Championship match on Wednesday was decided surprisingly swiftly; Abberley and Hemmings were left out, Lloyd and Oliver were brought in, primarily to give them the experience they need, because they are not yet necessarily better than those omitted.

I didn't feel it could be left just like that, and on my initiative Alan Oakman, John Whitehouse and I conducted private interviews with each of the players involved, explaining our reasons for the action and what we now expected of them. This process occupied most of the afternoon and, we felt, achieved enough to encourage us to interview every other member of the playing staff when next they were together, on Tuesday.

Monday July 24
Shopping for furniture occupied me; a seventh successive day
without cricket.

Tuesday July 25
An early-morning net, just forty minutes until the sun
brought up the moisture. This makes the wickets bouncy, and
too dangerous for practice. Then it was back to the far-
reaching business of seeing each player in turn, being critical
where necessary and encouraging when needed.

Some, naturally, were more difficult than others. Rebel occupied us for some while, as we explained to him that he must
get fitter. He is a burly guy with too much muscle for his own
good, but he isn't supple and he doesn't have the stamina to
support his considerable talent. He was told firmly, but con-
structively, just what he needed to do to realize his very considerable potential as a Warwickshire player. The uncapped
players were treated just the same, and it was three o'clock
when the last player departed from our interview room.

Talking to people like this will bring no overnight transitions, but it has at least established a communication; each individual had the opportunity to make his points just as we
made ours. I hope it was all worthwhile.

It is almost Test match time again, so I shan't be around to
study the new side just yet, and when I left the ground I
dropped in on Bernard Thomas to deliver my kit in readiness
for the trip down to London. The managerial appointments
for the tour of Australia have just been made, and it was an
obvious talking point for Bernard, who will once again ac-
company the team as physiotherapist cum general nursemaid.
The choice of Doug Insole as manager, ahead of Alec Bedser,
seems to have caused some surprise, but Bernard pointed out
that no one is better informed on the Packer situation than

Doug, and as such he must be a wise choice for this particular
tour. Kenny Barrington, manager of the last two tours, goes·
as assistant this time and will doubtless be left chiefly in
charge of team affairs while Doug handles the political side.
No complaints from me.

Back home, I climbed into bed at ten. Sleep, however, just
wouldn't come . . . and I turned once again to that hypnosis
tape.

8
England Beat
the Weather

Wednesday July 26

The Oval has never been my favourite ground. Jaundiced perhaps by my unhappy time with Surrey, I now have a subconscious dread of the wicket. It is, almost without exception, the
flattest, lowest wicket in England. In layman's terms, that
means a fast bowler can flog his heart out all day long and
never get a ball to deviate or rise above stump height. I often
find I feel more tired during an Oval Test than any other, and
I believe that is mainly psychological. I expect to have to work
harder here to achieve anything, so I expect to be tired. Consequently, I generally am.

The South London setting around The Oval is an insult to
the eye. I was brought up with all the great Surrey sides, and it
seemed natural that I should go there if I was to make a career
out of cricket. But the ground, overwhelmed by its hideous
gasholders and dirty riverside buildings, and suffering sometimes from lack of atmosphere, can in time erode enthusiasm
in the most eager player. I am glad I left when I did, for Warwickshire, despite the current transitional phase, can offer so
much more in most ways. All the same, despite the lack of
atmosphere at county matches, at Test time there is at least
the advantage of a good crowd inside the ground, and our current form, coupled with the unknown quantity of the New

Zealanders, should ensure a decent attendance for this Test.

Before checking in at The Oval, I had to go to Chelsea for another portrait sitting and a further fascinating chat with Theo Ramos. Afterwards he took me to his club in St James's Place, where I passed a happy hour or two before peeling off and heading for the ground. Almost as a formality, I checked the wicket, ascertained that it looked par for the course, and then gently loosened up in the nets.

New Zealand's tour has been plagued by injury worries already, but it seems they are willing to risk Richard Hadlee, their one penetrative seamer, despite his recent back injury. Talking of which, Scagg has a pinched nerve in his back, but in the present climate there is about as much chance of him withdrawing as of the Queen abdicating.

Spirit in the side is predictably high, but at tonight's team dinner, back above platform one at the Charing Cross Hotel, we were all prepared to admit that we expected a tougher fight against New Zealand than in the summer's first series. John Wright and Bev Congdon are both capable of long innings in an anchor role, Geoff Howarth seems in good form and already has two successive centuries against us, and the young left-hander Bruce Edgar has impressed all who have seen him. Their bowling strength, we decided, may rely rather too heavily on Hadlee.

Dinnertime talk was not confined to the match ahead. There is a strong move, prompted by myself, to employ an agent in Australia this winter. The commercial opportunities for our players promise to be vast, and with the Packer project in opposition it seems a good idea to control properly and exploit our market value. It is a scheme that promises to cause a few tremors at hierarchy level, but the seeds were sown among the players tonight and it received unanimous approval.

Not quite so unanimous was the approval given to the

rejection of proposals put forward by Kerry Packer at the International Cricket Conference meeting at Lord's which finished today. We all had the feeling that Packer was flying a kite, as the proposals were wildly ambitious. But while most of the England players are quite strongly against the entire World Series Cricket concept, there are exceptions, including Scagg, who is very much in favour of a compromise. This subject will no doubt occupy all those who go to Australia this winter.

Thursday July 27
I felt rough as soon as I had finished my exercises. Thinking that it may be a lack of energy after ten days without cricket, I took a salt tablet and promptly vomited my breakfast. It was a disturbing way to begin a Test match, and could only partly be put down to nerves. We lost the toss, which seemed a heavy blow, and I bowled without much venom throughout the day. Hard to explain why.

New Zealand began to justify our respect for them by reaching 130 for 1 in mid-afternoon, with Wright, who continues to bug me, and Howarth playing comfortably.

For the first time since I have known him, Mike Brearley came close to losing his cool on the field. Our cricket became lethargic and, particularly in the period leading up to lunch, we gave the impression of simply going through the motions. Scagg is too good a captain to let that pass, and I could see he was gritting his teeth to retain his composure. Before we took the field again after lunch, he had a go at us all in the dressing room. It was justifiable and effective, as we began to play with far more purpose during the remaining sessions.

The breakthrough, however, was almost handed to us by some very inept strokes. Wright and Howarth both got themselves out on the verge of very big scores, and the needless run-out of Bev Congdon in the evening left us in a far better position than we had the right to expect. New Zealand were seven wickets down for just over 200, and must have been desperately disappointed.

It was good to see Geoff Miller contributing at last. He bowled well today, in a long spell, and I encouraged Scagg to keep him on against Edwards and Hadlee when the new ball was due. Both these players are essentially hitters who prefer the seamers, and the ploy was successful.

Conversely, Phil Edmonds, our other specialist spinner, had a day he would wish to forget. His control disappeared and he suffered for it. Graham Roope uncharacteristically put down two simple catches and felt very down about it. He knows his Test place, and his chances of touring Australia, hang by a slim thread, and he probably feels he now needs a big innings more urgently than at any time in his career.

It could have been a day when the harmony of our dressing room was put to the test. We were on the rack for the first time this summer, and we were perhaps a little fortunate to come through so well.

Friday July 28
I woke soon after six to the sight of wet streets outside. It had rained in the night, and the wicket might have gained in life.

We fairly rapidly went through the remainder of the Kiwi batting, although I was frustrated by constant delays caused by spectators moving in front of the mock sightscreens. Even with spinners at both ends, it is difficult to reach the over-rate required to avoid a fine. The only solution is solid sightscreens on the boundary, but that would cause untold problems at The Oval, where the pavilion, and the members' seats, are directly behind the bowler's arm.

I felt a little stiff, and quite sore around the knee which I had injured yesterday. I needed some treatment while our batsmen made life difficult for themselves by playing one-day shots again.

Scagg was out for single figures again and this, I think, is the lowest ebb he has reached. Generally, Mike can be philosophical about dismissal, and after the few minutes of silent meditation that every batsman needs after being out, he is fairly cheerfully back amongst us. Today, things were different. He sat in his corner of the dressing room for about fifteen minutes, first staring at the floor and then studying a book. With the new make-up of the Oval dressing rooms, most of the players remain in a viewing area which is separated from the changing quarters by glass windows. It was some time before Mike rejoined us.

The reactions of other batsmen when they are out interested me today. Clive Radley was well in and around the 50 mark when an unnecessary risk got him run out. He came back fuming, furious only with himself for having thrown away a potential century. David Gower, who played well again, is among the quietest, while at the other end of the scale lie Ian Botham and Phil Edmonds. 'Guy' Botham is either extremely angry, or has an excuse. Being a restless, volatile individual, he rarely skulks for long and is very quickly chirping again. Goat has become known for saying something absurd when he comes in.

By the close tonight, the game was delicately balanced once again. Guy had got himself out to an ambitious sweep just before stumps, and only our tail remained to try and establish some sort of lead.

I left soon after the end to head for the BBC studios, where I was featuring in a late-night chat and music show hosted by Brian Matthew. Brian obviously knew a fair amount about cricket, and had done his homework, which was a relief to me. There is nothing more frustrating than an interview conducted by somebody who really doesn't know what he is talking about.

After the show, I went straight back to the hotel and had an unusually long soak in the bath, trying to ease away the physical aches. The Oval seems to be harder on the feet than any other ground, and it has certainly taken its toll on me.

Saturday July 29
'The train now standing at platform 5 . . .' brought me into the woken world at quite an early hour, cursing the noises of this hotel. Despite the supposed soundproofing, there isn't much goes on in the station below that we don't know about. The day dawned humid, and our fifty minutes batting at the start of play was a very sticky experience. I managed to hang around for a while with Goat and added some useful runs.

I enjoy batting, especially with the knowledge that nobody is allowed to drop the ball short at me. Like Pakistan's Sarfraz, I have a very long reach, and although I have never made a great deal of runs, my Test record proves that bowlers often find it difficult to get me out. Even for a number eleven, I have a very high proportion of not-outs.

The serious business of the day was in turning our first innings lead into a real advantage, and that was achieved quite spectacularly. By the end of the day we were once more on the verge of a Test victory in four days, after New Zealand had collapsed dreadfully.

I was very pleased to take the important wicket of Geoff Howarth before he had scored. 'Kiwi', as he is called by English friends, remains a very close mate of mine, but I am well aware that he likes to get off the mark with a fluent drive. With that in mind, I gambled with a deliberately overpitched, slow half-volley. It was wider than I intended it, but Geoff fell for the bait, drove – and edged the ball into his stumps for a calculated if slightly fortunate dismissal.

My bowling carried a lot more bite than it had done on the first day, but I was pleased to rest in the deep during the last session while Phil Edmonds – vastly improved from his efforts on Thursday – completed a very fine day with further important breaches. They were seven wickets down by the close, with only Congdon of the recognized batsmen left, and I felt justified in winding down and celebrating at a very enjoyable party in Purley.

Sunday July 30
Around midday, those players who have chosen to stay at the hotel rather than go home for the weekend, began to trickle into the bar. Geoff Miller, who can sleep for more than twelve hours most nights and looked as though he just had, arrived with hair tousled and eyes heavy. Ian Botham, who had been with me at last night's party, appeared slightly under the weather but elected to revive himself with a pint of lager. And Chris Old, the champion beer-drinker of the side, strode in sporting a T-shirt which proclaimed, 'I am an alcoholic. In case of emergency, buy me a pint.'

Sundays at a London Test match are nothing days. Unless you choose the tourist pursuits, there really isn't a lot to do, and the walks in the vicinity of Charing Cross are hardly inspiring.

Chilly, whose wife had come down for the weekend, had been to one of the Sunday street-markets – hence the T-shirt – and Dusty and Guy had decided to spend the afternoon at a benefit match in Berkshire. So after sharing a drink with them, I set off for Stoke d'Abernon and a quiet afternoon with Tannoy and Grummidge.

Watching what remained of a rain-ruined John Player League match on television, I wondered yet again just how much damage this sort of cricket might have done. When young players are forced to get used to slogging in limited-over games that can be even shorter than this particular 20-over farce, it is small wonder that few grafters in the mould of John Edrich are emerging on the scene.

By eight o'clock, I was back in the hotel. The hypnosis tape helped me to get to sleep, a welcome early night.

Monday July 31

The rain began just before the scheduled start, and soon after lunch, puddles, turning quickly into lakes, extended across the outfield from end to end.

I have seldom seen a ground so badly rain-affected. Play today was obviously out of the question, as the rain poured incessantly, and the umpires officially gave up hope soon after three o'clock. I fear that tomorrow must be in grave doubt already, which would leave us frustrated on the verge of victory.

Without any cricket to restrict my appetite, I would normally have got stuck into a sizeable lunch on a day like this. But it didn't quite work out like that. If only the catering at The Oval was as good as that at Lord's, where the friendly Nancy does such a marvellous job, I might really have enjoyed it.

A typical lunch menu for a Test day at Lord's would be: soup; roast lamb, roast potatoes and two vegetables; hot fruit pie and custard; variety of cheeses and biscuits; tea or coffee. For a drink with the main course, I usually have a glass of orange or lemon squash, certainly nothing stronger, and if possible nothing too fizzy, as I find that can upset me when I start bowling again.

Most of the England lads enjoy their food and eat heartily whenever possible. I say that because, for the bowlers at least, there are clearly occasions when to wade through a four-course lunch would be asking to be sick on the field. If we are bowling at the time, most of the seamers will stay in the dressing room and order something light and easy to digest. I normally choose cheese in a roll or sandwich – although at Edgbaston I have a slice of ham or tongue – and follow up with some plain ice cream.

Today we were at least able to dally at the table, compared with the normal rush to bolt our food in half an hour and be back in the dressing room in time to follow the umpires out. But with the rain lashing down outside, we were a fairly deflated bunch of players.

During the afternoon, the card school was opened again. But I wandered into the pavilion, where I met some old pals from Corinthian Casuals, the football team I used to play for. Among them was a girl, once the Casuals' secretary, and I took an immediate liking to her.

Tuesday August 1
In the early hours of this morning the rain finally ceased, but I woke with the conviction that I would be heading back to Birmingham as soon as the abandonment had been confirmed.

But a miracle had happened: the water had all disappeared, thanks partly to the extensive covers – borrowed from Lord's and Wimbledon – and the work of the ground staff since five in the morning, but chiefly, I think, to the remarkable drainage system under The Oval. Ten years ago a similar swamp had dried in a matter of hours to allow Derek Underwood to bowl England to victory and to The Ashes against Australia. Today, it was just as welcome.

When you expect to be sitting about for an early abandonment and a drive home, it is a strange sensation to find that you are exercising as usual and playing by eleven o'clock. For a while, it almost felt unreal.

Congdon and Cairns obviously had no such emotions, and for ninety minutes they resisted so stubbornly that escape seemed a possibility for New Zealand. Dusty finally broke through with the wicket of Cairns and, as so often happens, the rest folded almost instantly. We were left with a target of 138, plenty of time to get them, but with the forecasters predicting more rain spreading into London in late afternoon.

I was reminded of the Nottingham Test a year earlier, when what should have been a comfortable win over Australia became a race against time as rain reached Sleaford, only ten miles away from the ground. This time the rain had reached Thornton Heath, perilously close, but Graham Gooch's superb 90 not out steered us home.

The rest of the batting still doesn't convince me. Poor Scagg failed once more, David Gower got out to the sort of loose stroke he must learn to control, and Roopey, coming in near the end, survived without impressing.

The Kiwis came into our dressing room afterwards to share our champagne, proving again what a great-hearted side they are. I find it very hard to mix socially with the opposition after losing a Test, and they came in despite having a six-hour coach journey to Torquay ahead of them.

Before leaving the ground, I snatched a few quiet moments with Scagg, who confided that he had agreed to drop down the order to number five for the next Test. Geoff Boycott was to return and Graham Roope, as expected, would drop out. I hope Mike knows what he is doing, because if he fails again now, there is only one move left – and that is out of the team.

9
The Sacking of Amiss

Midway through the 1977 season, Dennis Amiss signed a contract with Kerry Packer. At a stroke, he ostracized himself within the Warwickshire club he had served faithfully and successfully for a decade and a half. The things he was to say and the agonies he was to put himself through in the twelve months to come convince me that he had not considered the possibility that his action could cut the throat of his county career and inevitably cause an adverse affect on his entire life.

This needs a retrospective explanation, because the Amiss story in 1978 was an ongoing one, re-emerging prominently at intervals. But at all times it concerned me more than almost any other player, because in September of 1977 I had rejected a similar offer from Packer. I didn't turn down his considerable financial inducement without great thought, but I came to the eventual conclusion that it would not be good for my personal career and that the entire Packer project would never benefit the average county cricketer.

The decision that I made, and my thinking behind it, perhaps caused me to become one of the leaders in the anti-Packer faction among county players. Naturally, this resulted in the straining of what had always been a friendly relationship between Dennis and myself. I was of the opinion that he could not have his cake and eat it — that he should never be picked for Warwickshire again. But the committee decided that such drastic measures, even if justified, were unwise in that they could certainly leave them open to legal reprisals. Instead they made it known that he would not be re-engaged once his contract had expired at the end of the 1978 season.

That might have been the end of the story . . . but it wasn't. Dennis Amiss is a very popular man in Warwickshire, and a large band of people were willing to support his fight to stay on. The episode rumbled on throughout the season but, looking back, it was in early August that the most significant moves were made.

Thursday August 3

To the fitting accompaniment of a tremendous thunderstorm, I wended my way to Edgbaston for another talk with Alan Smith; not, this time, about my own position but about Sacker's. The decision to dismiss him at the end of the current season had met with near unanimous support from the players, but a rather icy reception from some of the members. Due to their pressure, the committee may yet be forced to change their minds.

It is a situation brought about by Warwickshire members' loyalty to one of their own kind. Amiss was born in Birmingham in 1943, and has spent most of his life on the county staff. The sense of outrage that seems to have arisen is not because we are sacking a Packer player but because we are sacking a local Birmingham boy.

As for Dennis himself, he seems oddly bewildered by the anti-reaction of the men who were once friends as well as team-mates. I believe he feels particularly bitter about my attitude, as I have never disguised my view that he should not be in the side. Although he has not yet said so, Sacker could feel aggrieved because he has found himself in a tight corner, whereas I have done very well for myself out of turning down a Packer contract, with official Test fees promptly being boosted to £1000 per match by the Cornhill sponsorship.

I won't pretend that I lightly rejected the money that Packer offered me last August. It was a very difficult choice to make. Tony Greig made the initial approach to me during the final Test against Australia at The Oval. When I asked him for more details, he explained that I would be part of a World Eleven taking on the West Indian and Australian contingents. I immediately expressed doubts about my ability to motivate myself to play for 'a World Eleven' and Greigy's response was that the money would provide all the motivation anyone could need.

He had hit on the basic difference between us, for I could never be motivated to play cricket purely by money.

Despite this discouraging start, I spent several weeks thinking about the offer. To their credit, nobody on World Series Cricket hustled me in any way; I was left alone to make up my mind.

It is important to stress that I was always fully aware that to sign for Packer would probably mean the end of my county career. I didn't want that to happen, because Warwickshire had supported me like a crutch during the dark days when injuries rendered me almost useless to them. In 1975 and 1976, I played seven Championship games out of a possible forty. Yet they never lost faith in me. I owed them an awful lot for that.

It's true that I have done very nicely out of staying with the establishment, and I could not have hoped to be financially better off if I had signed. But my principles, I believe, were on a different wavelength to Sacker's.

Having opted to stay, I could not accept that anyone who chose the other route should still be welcome on the county circuit, where he would be taking the place of a player for the fuure. I didn't want to make an enemy out of Dennis. We had shared some happy times together; I used to dine with him quite regularly. But our relationship faded with a dreadful inevitability as the issue became bigger by the week.

Now, I fear, it is approaching confrontation time. If the committee stand firm and sack him, the members could easily revolt and overthrow them — and that would be a disaster for the county. Despite all its current faults on the playing side, Warwickshire is efficiently run by a carefully chosen all-purpose committee, and I should hate to see them broken up through making a bold decision.

Other counties, Kent and Somerset among them, have already stated that they intend to keep their Packer men on — which I think is disgraceful. But it does mean that we will be swimming against the tide if Amiss is fired, and that prospect understandably worries everyone. Alan explained all this to me today. I was disappointed, but I could see the reasoning behind his fears. For my part, I confirmed that the majority of players would back the committee if they went through with the dismissal.

Friday August 4
At lunchtime today, the senior Warwickshire players gathered in the bar of the White Swan for an informal discussion on Dennis Amiss's future. It may sound like the heads of the underworld getting together to draw straws. for the pleasure of carrying out the 'contract', but it was in fact a meeting inspired by genuinely strong feelings that something ought to be done. There may be nothing any of us can do to influence the final verdict, but it was a good idea to collate everyone's private opinions.

It didn't surprise me to learn that everyone felt the

committee should stick by their guns – defy the members if necessary – and sack him. What was more interesting was to hear the strength of Alvin and Barnsley's opinions – the two players who, along with me, have been involved more closely than anyone with Packer.

Like so many other players, Alvin signed for Packer at the time the 'circus' was being conceived, without really considering what damage it could do to his settled pattern of life. When he realized the truth he got out – helped by his existing contract with an Australian radio station. He gave up a great deal of money so that he could go on playing for the West Indies and Warwickshire, but now he sees Amiss taking the money *and* continuing his county career. Not surprisingly, he feels aggrieved. Alvin's cricket has been torn apart this summer by the shadow of Packer. Along with Barnsley and me, he was outspoken today ... but nobody argued against the judgement that Sacker must be dismissed.

Tomorrow, the politics must temporarily be put aside when we play Somerset at Weston – my first match for Warwickshire in three weeks. But although we made the effort to brighten the horizon by spending the afternoon and evening on the champagne terraces of Bibury Court, there was really no escape.

Saturday August 5
It was a great and pleasant surprise to me when the girl I had met among football pals at The Oval agreed to come to Weston for this weekend. She duly arrived soon after lunch, and is to stay with Mr and Mrs Botham in their second home here. It isn't like me to move this fast with any girlfriend. I am among the more strongly confirmed of the bachelor breed and in fact, during one of many idle hours on the Pakistan tour last winter, I accepted a wager to that effect.

It was Christmas time, and we were in Hyderabad. John Lever, my room-mate, was thoroughly unwell with the infamous 'Paki belly', and a bored Guy the Gorilla joined us in our room for a drink. Although only twenty-two, Guy is a happy husband and father, whereas JK and myself — both much older — are bachelors. As we talked, a bet was struck. Guy was willing to give a bottle of best Napoleon brandy to either JK or me if we weren't married within three years. At the time, I felt brashly confident of victory. But you can never be sure what will come along. . . .

The cricket today was depressing. By the end of it, we had dived to 90 for 9 on a wicket that contains very few evils.

Off the field, Alan Smith arrived and proceeded to take the senior players aside in turn to gauge their views on the Amiss front. I don't think he can have been left in much doubt as to the general reaction.

Horror films may upset some people, but the lunacy of the antique black-and-white ones normally cheers me up, so tonight, with our respective ladies having retired to bed, Guy and I enjoyed ourselves watching the late-night movie — *The House of Wax*. It made Warwickshire's strife seem slightly less real.

Sunday August 6
Black Sabbath again. We never threatened to get enough runs to defend in the day's John Player League fixture, and I can understand the lads' forlorn feelings as they go out each Sunday expecting another beating.

Monday August 7
Back to the Championship match, in which our innings limped into three figures on the back of my own contribution

of 23 not out – the highest score on our side. But although Chris Clifford bowled well and looks to be settling in and proving himself a good investment, once again we cannot hope to avoid defeat.

Tuesday August 8

The inevitable defeat was completed, after we had set them to score only 60 in the fourth innings – another wretched game for us. I have sympathy for John Whitehouse, however, as he has listened to all the points I had to make, and he is consulting his other senior players on the field.

The make-up of the team is planned with future success in mind, and we must hope that the promise shown by the batting of David Smith and Andy Lloyd in recent games is fulfilled over the closing weeks of the season.

It seems I have been back for scarcely any time at all, but tomorrow I return again to the Test scene, and while I leave for Nottingham, John Whitehouse will be handing in a statement from the Warwickshire players to the county committee. It was drafted to show our unified views about the Amiss situation, and its aim is to assure the committee that they have our support at least. I'm afraid we cannot hope to escape repercussions from members, though.

Driving back up the M5 from Weston to Birmingham, I was reminded once again just how much of the modern cricketer's life is spent on the road, and living out of a suitcase. I'm very lucky to have Big Sue to look after my laundry, for on evenings like these, all I have the time or energy to do is dump the dirty clothes and pack the clean ones. The problems of a bachelor . . .

10
Boycott Returns

Wednesday August 9

Just as he did twelve months ago, Geoffrey Boycott chose Nottingham to make his return to the England side. Last year, the gap had been four seasons; this time it is only four Tests. But although he was officially injured throughout this year's absence, the gossips and scandalmongers have been busy formulating their own theories on his reasons. Whatever Fiery does or says is news these days. That is a situation he has helped to bring upon himself, and I'm never sure how much he relishes the constant spotlight. I do think he now wants to play for England again; I am also sure that his runs will make us a far more complete team.

Before driving to Nottingham, I dropped into Edgbaston this morning to collect my mail. More requests for autographs, naturally, and it really does bemuse me. When I was at school, the great challenge was in meeting the player and asking him for his autograph face-to-face (I didn't collect. many simply because I was far too shy to approach a famous cricketer!). Autographs obtained through the post just didn't count at all.

On the outskirts of Nottingham, I stopped for a fish and chip lunch, and soon wished I hadn't. They were the worst I'd ever tasted. On to the ground with a nasty taste in my mouth.

By the time I arrived, Fiery had already had a long net, and was preparing to go in for another. His appetite for net practice is quite insatiable, but that is one thing that young players should never criticize. His record proves the value of it.

The Trent Bridge ground tends to produce as intimate an atmosphere as any in England. To many people it is a favourite ground, and it certainly has a very friendly charm. The dressing room entrance is on the right of a big brick pavilion, white-painted along its lower levels. Down a corridor and up two flights of stairs, the England (or home) quarters are on the second floor and consist of two large and airy rooms and a small ante-room which houses a wash basin and the junior players' lockers.

Last year, Fiery had set up camp alone in the ante-room and scored a century on his emotional comeback day. Whether through superstition, or simply because he prefers to have some solitude for his meditations, he was in there again today and obviously intends to settle there for the duration of the match.

Before we left the ground for the Albany Hotel, Bob Taylor and I were asked to a meeting with officials of the TCCB tomorrow night, at which the projected promotional contracts for the players in Australia will be discussed. Scagg would have been the obvious man to invite to the meeting, but I get the impression he is reluctant to embarrass himself by discussing tour matters when, in his own mind, he has not had the batting success to guarantee his place.

At tonight's team dinner, one of the major areas of concern was how I should set about bowling to John Wright. Most of the team expressed a view on whether I should continue over the wicket or attack him around the wicket with the aim of making him play the ball more; up to now he has shown a lot of skill and judgement in leaving the ball outside off stump. It was finally decided, with my approval, that I should experiment round the wicket, although, true to form, Phil Edmonds disagreed.

Thursday August 10
As soon as Geoff Howarth dropped Fiery early in his innings today, it seemed inevitable that he would get a hundred . . . and so it was to prove.

No matter what you think of this man, his concentration has to be admired. There were times out there today when he looked far below his best – he told us the ball was moving a lot all day – but his gaze never wavered from three figures and it never seemed possible that he would settle for less.

Batting had certainly not been easy in the early overs. The forecast was fine, but grey clouds thickly covered the sky. The swing bowlers were obviously going to benefit, but I doubt whether it seriously crossed Scagg's mind that we should gamble the toss on fielding first. He didn't, anyway.

Even before the start, two surprising events had occurred: John Wright withdrew from the New Zealand side, and John Lever did not turn up till about the time the players were taking the field. Wright declared himself unfit with flu on doctor's advice and thus deprived the New Zealanders of their most solid bat and me of the chance to test the theory that we had spent so long discussing last night. J K slept on in his hotel room after his early-morning call, and I can imagine his sheer panic when he woke at eleven o'clock, just half an hour before the start. The usual traffic jam across the River Trent delayed him still further, and he arrived at the ground at high speed and in a state of disarray. It was a unique lapse by a dedicated cricketer and just goes to prove that misfortune can overtake even the most careful at times.

Fortunately, JK knew already that he was to be twelfth man; had he been in the side, his panic would have reached still greater heights. As it was, he just suffered merciless mickey-taking all day long.

All the top batsmen made runs today, and Fiery's presence made the batting look immeasurably stronger. Every time he came off, he would retire to his private room and meditate for a while, before emerging to tell us what a difficult wicket it was to bat on. We were in no mood to argue. The Nottingham crowd took to him again, as they did last year, and he really does seem to be as much a folk hero here as he is further up the motorway in his native county. It will be interesting to compare the reaction that Scagg gets when he bats in his new number five position tomorrow.

I spent the day being alternately worried by my knee, which is still sore after my fall at The Oval, and amused by the antics of Guy, who becomes more bored and restless in the dressing room than anyone. He did manage to sleep for a while this afternoon, as did Hendo and Dusty, and all three awoke looking refreshed. I only wish I had the capacity to switch off and sleep when I felt like it.

When he wasn't sleeping, however, Guy was being a nuisance to all. His favourite trick at the moment is to stir his tea, then press the scalding hot spoon against somebody's bare arm. Rad was the sufferer today, and took his punishment well amid general hilarity. Guy has also devised a new nickname for Fiery — 'Thatch', as a reference to his much-publicized hair transplant. I'm pleased to say that Fiery accepted even that with a smile today, along with frequent cheerful insults from the irrepressible Botham.

Bob Chat and I left quickly after the close to attend our meeting. Doug Insole, retiring chairman of the TCCB, and Donald Carr, the secretary, were both there, along with selectors Alec Bedser and Ken Barrington, Jack Bannister of the Cricketers' Association and Peter Lush, the Board's promotions man. In principle, they all agreed that commercial representation for the touring players would be a good thing, if sensibly controlled. It is a measure of the businesslike progress made in the game over recent years, and particularly since Packer, that these administrators all accepted an idea which would have caused screaming and gnashing of teeth not so long ago.

The details remain to be arranged, but the provisional approval was encouraging. I fear, however, that the next part of the meeting will not be so eagerly applauded by the players.

In the dressing room earlier today, most of the talk had centred on Australia and the fact that we could probably expect another considerable increase in tour fees. Some were plainly naïve, assuming that because last year the fee was improved from £3000 to £5000, it would be right to hope for £7000 this time. The offer made by the Board is considerably less than that. They propose a flat ten per cent rise, but with an additional increase, from £100 to £200, for every previous tour a player has been on. This must be sensible, for it cannot be right that, for instance, a teenager like Paul Downton on his first England trip should earn as much as Geoff Boycott in Pakistan last winter.

Both Chat and I agreed that the offer was reasonable, but we fully expect to be in the minority when it is put to the team. What the others must remember is that a few years ago, cricketers were paupers; the sudden elevation to decent rates of pay is no excuse for further excessive demands by people who would struggle to earn anything near as much as their tour fee if they stayed in England for the winter.

Friday August 11

Lured by the inevitable sounds of Dylan blasting from my portable cassette player, Fiery poked his head round the door of my room at breakfast time. After displaying envy at my double bed, booked for me as usual by the TCCB at Lord's and one of the very few to be had in the Albany, he passed the time of day chatting about various things, and generally seemed pretty relaxed and happy, which is perhaps what you would expect from one who is unbeaten with more than 100 to his name.

Although I would never choose Fiery as a social partner for a night out, I can and do have a laugh with him when the mood is right. There are players who hate him for what he is and what he has done, but they don't include me in their number.

Recent years have transformed Fiery from the insular, bespectacled boy to the snappy dresser and confident and capable public speaker. He is a personality and he carries it off well, to the chagrin of his enemies. I will never feel as close to him as I do to Mike Brearley, but that is not to say I would always back Scagg's opinions. My views on Packer, for instance, coincide almost completely with Fiery's and clash just as comprehensively with Scagg's.

Fiery didn't add many more this morning before he was out hooking at his old adversary Hadlee, but we went on to a total of 429, featuring an agonizing half-century from Scagg.

The crowd's reception for him was half-hearted, but I think they began to live with him in his troubles. At first, he was scratchy, clearly tense and, to be frank, he didn't bat particularly well at any stage of his innings. He needed some luck, but after what he has been through recently, he was due for a large share. As he reached fifty, most of the team gathered on the balcony to applaud. It was a genuine gesture of real pleasure for the man who has bound the side together. At the same moment, one floor down, I'm sure the selectors were smiling broadly in their own private box; their man had done enough for his name to be inked in, rather than pencilled, as tour captain this winter.

Scagg was clearly relieved when he came in, although he knew very well that it hadn't been a great innings. Handshakes and backslaps were in order, and Fiery was among the first to congratulate him. No doubt feeling more assured about his own position, Scagg sat down with me to discuss the Australian tour, and particularly my own theory that we should take only one specialist wicketkeeper, which would leave room for an extra batsman. It's an interesting thought, possibly a workable one, but it may be decided that the risks might outweigh the advantages.

In late afternoon we were on the field for the first time, and Guy and Hendo made vital breakthroughs in the final session. The most significant delivery was also the saddest, as Guy made one rise sharply and Howarth, ducking ineffectually, took a nasty bump on the head. He was helped off by Nottinghamshire's female physiotherapist, whose sudden appearance on the ground persuaded many to think she was an angry woman brandishing her handbag to attack Guy. Kiwi Howarth was taken to hospital as a precaution and, if he can't come back to bat tomorrow, New Zealand's batting – already without Wright – will begin to look thin.

I spent the evening with the Edmonds-Botham duo, who had already got their arguments under way during an amusing afternoon game of 'Mastermind'. I'm not sure who won but I think they both claim to have done. At dinner tonight, their subjects for debate – always loud, often fierce and sometimes embarrassing – ranged from the Catholic religion to the merits of house wine, and inevitably they joined forces to hurl light-hearted abuse at Fiery, who was eating at the next table.

Saturday August 12
It was a bleak morning, the sky thick with threatening grey

cloud and the light appalling. The wicket, according to regulations, had been covered overnight, but as soon as play
began it would have to remain uncovered until stumps were
drawn for the night. Against that background, none of us
could envisage play starting on time, when the rain could fall
at any time and turn the open wicket into a treacherous trap
for the Kiwis.

I was so confident of an idle morning that I was watching
Laurel and Hardy on the television in the dressing room, and
had no boots on, when someone said that the umpires were
going out. In the consequent flap to get dressed for play, I
heard one facetious remark that was to stick in my mind. 'I
hope we bowl one ball before it pours with rain,' said whoever
it was. His wish was almost granted, as we squeezed in two
balls before the already gloomy light became completely impossible, and hurried us back to the pavilion.

I came off behind the New Zealand captain Mark Burgess,
and he was undoubtedly furious as he stalked into his dressing
room. I could understand his anger, for at the very least it is
desperately unlucky for a team to be exposed to such a disadvantage as this.

Play didn't begin again until after three o'clock, when we
swiftly discovered that the rain had not affected the pitch as
much as we might have hoped. I didn't bowl too well, but Guy
was magnificent once again. He is such an improved bowler
that he can still be devastating when the conditions give him
no help at all. New Zealand dived to 120 all out, more than
300 behind, and survived a single, hair-raising over from Guy
when they followed on just before 7.30. They are in a hopeless
position, and only further rain can logically rob us of another
victory to clinch the series.

My girlfriend had arrived this afternoon and, as arranged,
we set off for South Humberside with the Bothams to spend
the rest day at their real home in Epworth, a tiny village

where Guy can indulge his hobbies of shooting, fishing and golf. Tonight, however, we followed up *The House of Wax* at Weston by watching *The Incredible Shrinking Man*. We seem to be getting hooked on horror.

Sunday August 13
The perfect Sunday off. At 11.55 a.m., Guy and I set off for his favourite local pub, where we shared a pint or two with the friendly regulars. Then it was back to another pub, where we met the girls, and home for a feet-up doze in front of the television, followed by a splendid meal and an early night.

We agreed to stay up in Epworth tonight rather than drive back to Nottingham, and I felt more relaxed about everything than I've done for some time.

Monday August 14
New Zealand made far more of a fight of their second innings than their first, but the champagne was still flowing by six o'clock – our third four-day win of the season, or our fourth if you take off the washed-out day at The Oval.

Two daft run-outs typified the New Zealanders' plight. Anderson was so eager to get off the mark that he tried to run one off my bowling to mid-off, but David Gower's throw beat him easily. Then, after a good recovery, John Parker slipped, having come out after a shower of rain without spikes in his boots. It looked certain that we would be taken into a fifth day at one point, but the tail fell away rapidly and I do believe they are starting to look almost as dispirited as the Pakistanis.

The ease with which we have won this series has surprised everyone, and the only excuse the Kiwis can offer is that Hadlee has not yet been fully fit for a Test. I don't think there was much wrong with him here, but psychologically he still didn't feel ready to put everything into his bowling. Their back-up bowlers are short on menace.

A Test that began with thoughts of Boycott ended on a similar note. A crate of champagne had arrived in the dressing room, and Fiery, like everyone else, assumed it was a gift for the team. Only when it had been shared around, and much of it consumed, was it discovered that the crate belonged to Fiery as the *Sunday Telegraph's* Cricketer of the Week. I can't say he was pleased, but a phone call to the paper apparently produced another crate for his personal use.

II
Three out of Three

The days following victory at Nottingham were refreshingly quiet. Instead of driving home, I decided to visit friends in Bradford, and spent two days up there before returning to Birmingham.

They were pleasant days, away from the pressures of the season. I visited the pub run by former England batsman Peter Parfitt on Tuesday lunchtime, then spent the entire evening watching television – something I haven't done for more than a year.

Complete escape was impossible. On Wednesday morning, meandering through the Bradford shops, I was spotted and recognized by a girl assistant in British Home Stores, and obliged to sign some autographs. I found it rather embarrassing, but it is part of the job and can't be shirked.

Braced by the rest, I felt ready to throw myself back into the worries of Warwickshire.

Thursday August 17
Whenever the outdoor nets are not fit at Edgbaston, the matting wickets at the Warwickshire indoor school are available to us. That was the case today, but while most of the lads took advantage of the indoor facilities, I preferred to lap the Colts ground alone. Hard outdoor wickets will take their toll of fast

bowlers' feet and shins, but I find the indoor wickets even more punishing and always try to avoid bowling on them.

After lunch at the White Swan, I went to see Jim Cumbes, who had some news. He is thinking of taking a pub, and the only drawback in his mind is that it would mean giving up county cricket completely, which would be a tremendous wrench for one who enjoys it as much as he does. He has spent much of his active sporting life giving cricket second best to his career as a goalkeeper. Now that he has retired from football, he had hoped to devote more time to Worcestershire cricket for a few years – and the chance of a new life as a landlord is dragging his loyalties in all directions.

Leaving him to his decision-making, I joined David Smith and Phil Oliver for the evening, and listened to their opinions on the current situation at the county. Their views differed little from mine, and their observations were interesting coming from young and promising players. The next few weeks could be vital for these two, and I hope they make a go of it. Smithy needs to make the opener's position his own and justify the decision to play him regularly; Ollie must decide which direction he is going. He started the season bowling seamers and has now turned to cutters with some success.

I like both these lads and get on tremendously well with them, although they have contrasting characters and backgrounds. Smithy came down from Newcastle to play for us and is very close to Steve Perryman through having lived with Steve and his mother for some time. He is a dedicated batsman, who has learned the habit of writing off every wicket as being difficult to bat on. But he is a conscientious trainer who has got himself very fit, and he deserves success now.

Friday August 18
More nets at Edgbaston. They get harder at this time of year,

when some of us subconsciously believe we have bowled enough in matches not to need them, but I had a long bowl this morning and felt better for it.

An unexpected visitor at home this afternoon was Rohan Kanhai, who left us at the end of last season. He was not always the easiest man to get on with during his time at Edgbaston, but there is no doubt that we miss his runs.

Saturday August 19

The Warwickshire committee issued a statement early this morning, confirming that their original decision not to re-engage Dennis Amiss after the current season had ended was still valid and would be carried out. Cyril Goodway, the chairman, added some emotive remarks of his own, explaining that Warwickshire felt they should carry a banner against the 'scourge', as he called Packer, even if nobody else would.

Most people at Warwickshire feel betrayed and dismayed by the actions of counties such as Kent in reversing their earlier decisions on Packer players, and our committee was clearly in no mood to be swayed by the inevitability of angry responses from members. Reaction didn't take long to set in. A few season tickets were hurled into the secretary's office by disgruntled members, while the action group set up to get Amiss reinstated promise further moves. There is already talk of an extraordinary general meeting of the club to resolve this matter.

Dennis himself obviously feels resentful towards most of the other players, and the atmosphere in the dressing room today was tense. When he was out, Sacker sat in his corner writing letters on World Series Cricket notepaper. Not many words were spoken either by him or to him. It's all very unfortunate and I wish that scenes such as this could have been avoided.

Surprisingly, considering the action off the field, we turned in one of our best day's work this season and put ourselves in a very strong position against Sussex. We lost the toss, but bowled well on a slow and unresponsive pitch. I blasted four out, and Ollie's spinners claimed two in successive balls just before lunch. Sussex were out for 199, and by the close we had reached 120 for 3 with Smithy making strides towards the fulfilment of potential we all want from him. He has passed 50 and is still there.

Sunday August 20

One of the rare events of the season – Warwickshire won a John Player League match. We beat Sussex comfortably to keep alive our faint chance of honours – or, should I say, of finishing higher than last.

The Sussex team is so full of Surrey old boys that I feel quite at home in their company. They are led by Arnold Long, who was the wicketkeeper in my time at Surrey, and they also include Geoff Arnold, all-rounder Stewart Storey and Chris Waller, who regularly used to give me a lift from my parents' house to The Oval in the days before I had a car of my own.

We all seem to enjoy talking about the old days at Surrey far more than we actually enjoyed playing there!

Monday August 21

Entertaining is not the word I would choose to describe it, but David Smith's 130 not out today pleased me as much as any other innings I have seen this season. Smithy kept his head down through the morning after we had lost a couple of early wickets and Sussex were threatening to bowl us out for about the score that they made. On a wicket that began to turn a little for both Waller and Barclay, he showed Boycott-like application and scored at barely above one run an over. Considering the circumstances, and the overs we had in hand, it was just the sort of batting we needed from him, and it earned us a valuable lead of about 100.

When we went back in the field in our bid for an encouraging win, for various reasons we made little progress, and we may have let them off the hook.

I devoted the evening to buying dinner for Barnsley and his wife Cleo, which is really small repayment for the amount of times in a season they feed me at their farmhouse home. They are lovely people and great company. Barnsley's humour coincides with my own, which explains why we spend so much time together off the field. The most wholehearted trier any captain could ever wish for, he is probably happier now that he does not have the onerous task of being captain, and is still a very fine seam bowler. I dread the day when he gives up.

Tuesday August 22
Rain, growing in intensity as the morning progressed, made any play unlikely, and a phone-call from my lady, inviting me to come down to London tonight – a day before I have to report for the final Test – provided the lift I needed.

In the event, there was no play, so I went in search of 'Tiger' Smith, the great ex-Warwickshire player. He is ninety-two now but never misses a day of a home game, and I found him in his usual spot in the players' dining room, where he can sit in warmth and comfort while being plied with cups of tea. For a man of his advanced age, Tiger is amazingly shrewd about the county as it is today. Very little bypasses him, and he talked a great deal of sense as we sat and watched the rain come down this morning. Most significantly, he wondered whether the ability of some of our youngsters is being maximized. Much more should be got out of them.

At 4.30, I said goodbye to all the old friends in the Sussex side and headed for London, and the girlfriend's flat near Streatham Hill, where I used to share a flat in 1970. A shade of nostalgia crept up on me as I noticed the 109 and 133 buses dawdle past – the same buses that used to take me to The Oval all those eventful years ago.

Wednesday August 23
For the last time in a summer of overwhelming success, England's players gathered at Lord's this afternoon. But the occasion was not one for looking back. I don't think there was a player in the team whose thoughts were not firmly fixed on securing his ticket on the plane to Australia in two months' time.

John Emburey is the new boy – the only new cap we have introduced since David Gower in the first Test of the summer. 'Ernie' is Phil Edmonds's spin partner at Middlesex and obviously a fine off-break bowler. But at this stage I feel that his inclusion could leave the team with a dangerously long tail. Dusty, who has been left out to accommodate him, has not made many runs this season, but at least he is always capable of fifty.

Nets were gentle and our third Charing Cross dinner of the year was relaxed and confident. Nobody doubts any longer that we are comfortably New Zealand's superiors, and because of that, we didn't even bother with our customary dissection of the opposition. There didn't seem any point.

My sympathies tonight are with my great mate, JK. He is in the squad again, but knows that he can expect to be nothing more than twelfth man. And while he is fetching and carrying for the rest of us here, his Essex team-mates are playing the crucial Championship match against Kent in their bid to win something for the first time. JK's feelings must be very mixed, but knowing him as I do, he would never complain about being in an England twelve.

The phone next to my bed rang at eleven o'clock. It was Arnold Long, asking for tickets for the game. Normally, I would have been only too happy to help, but for some reason tickets for this match are like gold dust, and my daily allowance of four is nowhere near enough to cover the requirements of family and friends.

Thursday August 24
The season may be ending and the series decided, but I don't feel any less nervous. Apart from the game, there seem to be so many things to worry about: getting from the hotel to the ground across London, getting enough tickets for everyone, hoping that my sore knee stands up to bowling.

It transpired that I wasn't the only one panicking about tickets, and the dressing room table became a pre-match trading post, with somebody offering lunch and tea tickets and wanting admission tickets, somebody else wanting the opposite. Eventually I think everyone sorted themselves out, and we were actually ready to get on with the game.

Scagg lost the toss and we were duly condemned to the field on a fine morning and what looked a very good wicket. I proceeded to bowl two spells that I would rather forget very quickly. I could not find my length at all, and I honestly can't remember ever bowling so badly for England . . . which was not a good way to begin the last major match of a season in which I have bowled at my best.

We did squeeze five of them out by the close, which was a reasonable effort in unfavourable conditions, but it was clearly New Zealand's day, my old pal Geoff Howarth fighting off the effects of flu to score a brave century. We dropped him twice, which was odd in a year when England's fielding has been one of the features of our success, but the fact remains that we certainly face a battle to win this one.

Friday August 25
One of the fascinations of Test cricket is that one bad day does not rule you out. The next day can swing the game entirely the opposite way. Up to a point that is what happened today. True, New Zealand made 339 and we are still some way behind. But Ian Botham's bowling, and a combination of Clive Radley and David Gower with the bat, have put us in a far more promising position than I thought likely this morning.

Guy was brilliant again; another virtuoso bowling performance to hustle out the New Zealanders' low order. He finished with six wickets, which is scarcely exceptional by his own standards this year.

We couldn't have had a worse start. Hadlee was fit and confident at last, and he brought the first ball rearing up to take Graham Gooch's glove and spoon just wide of the short-leg. His second ball was almost a replica, only this time short-leg made the catch. Just before tea, we also lost Fiery. He had scored 24 and looked totally in command against some very hostile fast bowling indeed. Then, quite uncharacteristically, he followed one outside off stump and was caught.

His reaction was interesting, and showed that he has changed and matured as an individual. In the old days, he would have hidden himself away for hours without talking to anyone, but today, after just a few minutes alone, he got up and started talking about it. He was understandably bemused at having got out to such a wide ball, and for some time he wouldn't stop discussing it. He asked for different people's opinions of the dismissal, kept playing the shot again, as if to reassure himself that it wasn't such a blunder after all. Having done all that, he sat down again and started ploughing through the piles of autograph sheets and cricket bats left in the dressing room. Fiery is always one of the most conscientious about signing everything that is brought in.

I lounged on one of the antiquated sofas while we batted, and asked Bernard Thomas to look at my knee once again. As if one injury wasn't enough of a worry, I have now damaged a ligament on the outside of the same knee while bowling. It isn't painful enough to cause too much concern, however, and Bernard's advice is that I will be all right to bowl in the second innings.

Just as the day seemed to be fading out with the New Zealanders still on top, the two men we now call Lulu and Grizzly launched into one of the most spectacular partnerships of the summer. They took the Kiwis apart in the final ninety minutes, both batting quite superbly in their different styles. Grizzly will never be a stylist as long as he lives. He is in the mould of David Steele, though much more adaptable, and all the familiar short-arm drives, cuts and scoops were flowing tonight. The classical batting came from the other end, with a young man continuing his meteoric rise to stardom, and taking everything in his quiet and unassuming way as if it might all end tomorrow.

Saturday August 26
Collapse set in, our tail was proved to be too long as I had feared, and we were all out for 289 – forced to come from behind for the first time this summer.

As we prepared to take the field, Scagg made what was to become one of the quotes of the season. 'Look,' he said to his assembled team, 'If we get stuck in, we are capable of bowling this lot out for less than a hundred'. As prophecies go, it looks like being a classic. By close of play, the Kiwis had staggered to 37 for 7.

Ray Illingworth had had a chat with Scagg and suggested that he gave Ian Botham the new ball. He took his advice, putting Guy on at the nursery end and leaving me to bowl at the so-called ridge, which seemed to have given Hadlee's bowling so much more menace. The change in my bowling was extraordinary. On Thursday I had felt tired and low; yesterday, although I bowled better, something vital was absent. But everything clicked tonight. It was one of those joyous occasions in a fast bowler's life when every muscle of his body seems to be functioning smoothly. I bowled as quickly as I have ever done in my life, and blasted out Anderson, Congdon and the nightwatchmen Bracewell and Boock.

Geoff Howarth, still suffering with flu, didn't come out to bat; when he does it may be too late to make much difference.

We proved today that we have the tenacity to fight back — that we are not just a fair-weather side.

Sunday August 27
Another restful Sunday. My girlfriend and I played at tourists, lunching on the Old Caledonian floating pub, walking through the park to Speakers' Corner and visiting the Henry Moore exhibition. I enjoyed every minute of it.

Guy and his wife were with us again; a different Guy from the one we all know in the dressing room — a thoughtful and happy family man here. It occurred to me again that, at twenty-two years old, he has set himself up better than any cricketer in the game's history. My only fear for him is that his interminable chasing up and down the country, between his homes in Weston and Epworth, may eventually get him down. I could do it at twenty-two, but I couldn't now.

Monday August 28

It's over. The last Test of the summer ended well within its fourth day, and England had whitewashed New Zealand.

Their last three wickets put up no more opposition than we expected. I bowled very fast again and finished with four wickets. Guy took five – eleven in another incredibly successful match.

Umpire Dickie Bird gave me a warning for over-use of the short ball. I was a bit surprised as I had only bowled four bouncers in six overs at Geoff Howarth . . . but then my views on the bouncer are well known.

Before we went out, Scagg took some unmerciful stick for the very unimpressive new haircut he appeared with. I think he washed it before going out, just to see if it made it look any better! The whole atmosphere in the side was genial. Everyone gets on well in this team; there is no bitchiness, no personality clashes. It's so much easier when you are winning, of course, but I get the feeling that our spirit is pretty permanent.

Not that we won without a scare today. Hadlee bowled two superb deliveries in succession to castle Fiery and Grizzly, and our target of 116 suddenly looked a long way off. But two young and inexperienced Test players, Gooch and Gower, played magnificently with the pressure on them. Gower was totally uninhibited, and left in the glorious manner – a blinding drive caught at gully just as it seemed he would reach 50 to carry us home. I was pleased, though, that his dismissal got Scagg out to the middle. He only had time to score eight not out, but it was fitting that he was there at the death, which, ironically, was provided by a no-ball bowled by Hadlee.

Bob Taylor was named 'Man of the Series' by Jim Laker, and I don't think he could have made a better choice. Guy and Lulu may have been the spectacular stars, but Chat has kept wicket so well that nobody has even mentioned the name Alan Knott.

The New Zealanders came into our dressing room for drinks once again, and I really don't think any other side could have taken three heavy defeats as well as they have. They must be desperately disappointed, especially having beaten us in one Test on their own territory this year, but the plain truth is that they didn't have enough top-class players.

Almost immediately after the game, Alec Bedser appeared, beckoned to Scagg and took him off into the loo outside the dressing room – a salubrious spot to tell him officially that he would be England's captain this winter. Fiery will be disappointed, but I can't think of any England player who will not be delighted by the news.

With the formality of the appointment out of the way, Scagg sat down with Bob Chat and myself to sort out our ideas on a sixteen-man party for the tour. We finally all agreed that experience in the batting was what we needed, and suggested names of seasoned campaigners such as Steele, Lloyd and Fletcher as the extra batsman.

So there it is. The end of six Tests, five victories and a lot of very fine cricket played by England. Despite all the success, the summer lacked the sparkle of the Ashes, or a series against the West Indies . . . and we know the sternest tests are yet to come.

12
The Team for Australia

Tuesday August 29

Ten days remain of the county season – two Championship matches and one John Player League fixture. As ever at the tail end of a barren season, everyone has some trouble in maintaining a peak of application and determination.

Several players, however, have enough to prove to make it worth their while ... and the first and most obvious man springing to my mind is one who has been such a central character since I began this diary, Dennis Amiss. Whether through bravery or sheer obstinacy, Dennis will still admit to nobody – least of all himself, I suspect – that Warwickshire's announcement on his dismissal signalled the end of his career at Edgbaston. He probably convinces himself that by making more and more runs, he will persuade everyone at the club that he is indispensable. As expected, a group of Warwickshire members have exercised their prerogative and called a special general meeting to seek Sacker's reinstatement. Meanwhile, the man himself will bat on and on in search of 2000 runs for the summer.

At the other end of the scale, there is Andy Lloyd, who has won a batting place recently and should, with Amiss's departure, be an automatic choice for the start of next season – always providing that he does not let himself down in these closing games. The same applies to David Smith, establishing himself as a first-team opener, and hopefully to Phil Oliver in the middle order. As I said right at the start of the season, these lads are Warwickshire's future. I hope they realize that.

It was with these thoughts filling my head that I drove to Cardiff this evening for the penultimate Championship match, against Glamorgan. As usual I am sharing a room with Barnsley (unlike England and most of the other counties, every Warwickshire player, including the captain, has to share rooms), and when he arrived soon after ten, I was already in bed.

Wednesday August 30
The wicket at Sophia Gardens looked slow and dead, and a chat with the groundsman confirmed my worst fears. 'What did you expect?' he asked mischievously. 'I knew you were coming.' If it was useless to the quick bowlers, however, it certainly seemed to suit Mr Amiss, who showed just the dogged determination I had expected in scoring 160 – runs that will probably be more helpful to us in this match than to his cause in the long term.

With Barnsley nipping in for two early wickets in our short evening spell in the field, we ended the day handily placed to challenge for precious points in a belated bid to salvage some respect from our Championship position. There is no chance at all of us finishing within reach of the prize money for the top three handed out by Schweppes, but there is a little thing called pride which spurs on every team in our position.

Thursday August 31
More hope for the future came in the performances of our two spinners, Oliver and Clifford, who delivered a total of

seventy-one overs today, and did so impressively enough to hint that we might have a bit of range in our attack at last.

Friday September 1
A game that we had controlled for more than two days slipped away from us this afternoon – almost to the point of defeat. We batted reasonably well again and set Glamorgan to make 286. After their success in the first innings, I thought the spinners might well bowl them out, but it didn't work out that way. Glamorgan lost eight wickets, but came very close to pulling off a win.

While we were batting, I paid a visit to the National Sports Centre down the road and found myself fascinated by my first sight of women playing lacrosse. It looked both skilful and dangerous, and I made a mental note never to try it.

At about the time that I was leaving Cardiff to drive back to Birmingham, the England team to tour Australia was being picked behind the locked doors of a private room in London's Victoria Sporting Club, and about twenty-two cricketers around the country – all with reasonably well-founded hopes of selection – were beginning one of their most nervous weekends of the year.

Saturday September 2
The phone rang early and I guessed right. It was Scagg. Yes, I was to be vice-captain; yes, he had almost got the squad that he wanted. So the news was good. Looking through the tour squad, it seems certain to be a happy bunch. Almost all of us have toured together before during the past two years, and I can see no problems with the few newcomers, Graham Gooch, David Gower and John Emburey. All three are fairly quiet characters, but there is nothing obstructive or malicious in any of them.

And the vice-captaincy . . . yes, that is very good news. I must, of course, brace myself for the repercussions from the pro-Boycott brigade, who will undoubtedly be both outraged and mystified as to why their man has been overlooked. Most of them, however, have never been in a position to know Geoff's two sides, and although I admire him immensely, I would not like him to captain England. I know most of the other players feel the same, and it seems the selectors agree. Fiery is too obsessed with his batting to apply himself fully to the needs of the team. If he fails with the bat while leading the side, as happened more than once in New Zealand earlier this year, he tends to brood on his own disappointment to the temporary exclusion of the team. It is to everyone's advantage that he should be left to do what he does best – and that is score centuries – without extra burdens on his time and concentration.

For me, the job is an honour I prize highly. There are those who will say that, as a strike bowler, I am not in the best position to captain a side, but I don't necessarily agree. I also think that I have reached the stage in my career when a little more responsibility can only be a good thing, and I believe I have the respect of the players, so necessary if the job is to be carried out properly.

My duties on the field will naturally be to assist Scagg, and to lead the side when he rests. Between games, one of my most important tasks will be to organize the net practices, deciding who should bat next, who should bowl, when the slip fielders should peel off for catching practice etc . . .

The other unwritten task of the vice-captain is always to be available to listen to the grouses and the problems of other players. Those who are left out of a game often like to make their point to someone in authority, without turning it into an official protest by complaining to the captain. And those who consistently fail to make the Test team can often eventually become bored, irritable and homesick. It will be my job to alleviate these difficulties as much as possible. A tour can be lonely and depressing if things go wrong.

The strictest sorts of discipline, such as curfews and drinking restrictions, don't generally need impressing on England cricketers. In my experience, all but a wayward few have been sensible enough to know their own limitations and act accordingly. But there may come a time on tour when something stronger has to be said or done and, depending on the severity of the situation, the vice-captain may again be called upon.

If I'm making the tour sound suspiciously like a school outing, well, there are similarities. Everyone is told exactly what is expected of them each day; if we are travelling, we all know what time our bags should be left outside our rooms, what time we should have breakfast and what time we should report in the hotel lobby. Tickets, passports and luggage are all taken care of – all the careless cricketer has to remember is his own body. In terms of organization, everything is almost regimentally precise – as it needs to be to avoid accidents, and to ensure the necessary smooth conduct of any major tour.

When any tour team is announced, someone somewhere is disappointed – and normally it is not just one but half a dozen. The unlucky men are David Bairstow, the Yorkshire wicketkeeper who has missed out for the deputy's place after being hotly tipped for the third year in succession, and Kent's Chris Tavaré, who was apparently almost every journalist's choice for the place which might have gone to Steele but finally went to Randall.

Roger Tolchard, probably an inferior keeper to Bairstow, slipped in ahead of him on the strength of his positive, combative batting, which alone won him Test caps in India two years ago when Alan Knott kept wicket and 'Tolly' fielded at short-leg!

Tavaré, who obviously has time in front of him, missed out to Randall in what must have been a close-run thing. But Arkle is such a fun bloke to have on the tour, and I only hope he treats the Aussies to a few more innings like his century at Melbourne two years ago. If he doesn't, he will find himself branded as a flash in the pan.

Scagg and I talked for some while about the team and the tour, and reached the conclusion that something needs to be done about fitness well before departure date. We thought several were somewhat overweight and one or two needed to concentrate more on their overall fitness. Bernard Thomas is likely to be consulted to draw up training tips for each one of the tourists.

Once out in Australia, of course, we all come under Bernard's supervision for daily training. But it is vital that the players don't let their fitness slip in the intervening weeks. I have heard too many say that they intend to do nothing but relax until the tour, but however pleasant that thought may be, it isn't practical.

If it was down to me, I would assemble the entire tour squad a week before departure date, and devote the extra time in England to fitness training, a few nets to shake off the cobwebs and the crucial matter of assessing everyone's ability to live and work as a 'family' team. Four months is a long time for sixteen men to spend in each other's constant company, and it is best to be aware of any problems before setting off.

I appreciate that this will probably never be adopted. As a bachelor, it would be easy for me to give up the extra week, but on most tours the vast majority of the team are married and would baulk at the idea of a premature end to the one holiday period they can snatch during the year.

This year, in fact, five of the team are bachelors – Boycott, Gower, Lever, Tolchard and myself. The full squad which will be announced from Lord's on Monday is as follows:

Mike Brearley (Middlesex, captain), Bob Willis (Warwickshire, vice-captain), Ian Botham (Somerset), Geoff Boycott (Yorkshire), Phil Edmonds, John Emburey (both Middlesex), Graham Gooch (Essex), David Gower (Leicestershire), Mike Hendrick (Derbyshire), John Lever (Essex), Geoff Miller (Derbyshire), Chris Old (Yorkshire), Clive Radley (Middlesex), Derek Randall (Nottinghamshire), Bob Taylor (Derbyshire), Roger Tolchard (Leicestershire).

It is a team picked somewhat in the dark, because most of us know next to nothing about the 'new' Australian side since Packer stripped them of the Chappell generation of players. At a guess, there may be only two players in their Test side whom I have ever met before at international level. But Australia will never be written off. As usual, of course, they will produce someone to worry us . . . and it will probably be another fast bowler nobody has heard of – just as, on our last full tour there four years ago, they sprung one J.R. Thomson on us!

Sunday September 3
Sundays, as I have explained, rate pretty low in the Warwickshire popularity poll this season, but I can't recall one that I would like to forget more hastily than this. In typical Warwickshire fashion we managed to lose to the John Player League wooden-spoonists, and in very inglorious circumstances for our opening bowler! The match was meaningless and totally unmemorable, but for the fact that it was finished by Alastair Hignell hitting me for two sixes into the stand. Fortunately, Gloucestershire were already entrenched without hope beneath us, but to end with defeat against them rather summed up our summer of Sundays . . . or Black Sabbaths!

Monday September 4
Barnsley woke me at 6.30 this morning on his way to London
. . . for yet another top-level meeting on the Packer players!
The Cricketers' Association want to gauge the strength of the
players' feelings as quickly as possible now. If it is left to next
April, when everyone reconvenes for a new season, the World
Cup will almost be upon us – and a snap decision will have to
be made on whether England will play against Pakistan and
the West Indies, who are both likely to include their Packer
men.

At the start of this season, many county cricketers would
have supported a complete Test and county ban on World
Series players. It will be interesting to see if feelings have
softened. Mine certainly have not.

Tuesday September 5
At two o'clock today, the Warwickshire squad reported for
nets, which to me seemed slightly ludicrous on September
5 . . .

Wednesday September 6
A touch of déjà vu . . . a rainy morning and no play before
lunch – just like April and May all over again.

Took the opportunity to breakfast in style at The Towrope
and returned for the afternoon start against Derbyshire to
find myself bowling with an Australian 'Kookaburra' ball.
Each county is having to use these balls a certain number of
times this season as an experiment. Personally, I think it's a
failure, but then I might be influenced by the fact that I can't
get a wicket with them. They all seem to be soft, losing their

bounce after a few overs and their shape soon afterwards. Spectators often barrack when a fast bowler complains about a ball to the umpires, but they can't realize just how important it is to have one that stays hard and keeps its shape.

After close of play, Bernard Thomas, Bob Taylor and I met TCCB chiefs Doug Insole, Donald Carr and Peter Lush for further discussions on the proposed commercial sponsorship in Australia. It was an extremely progressive meeting, and I left it feeling how extraordinary it all was. Two years ago, I wouldn't have given these proposals a chance.

Bob Chat and myself went for a meal afterwards and lapsed into nostalgic talk about old times on tour. Many is the time that I've shared rooms with Chat, and I can't think of anyone more friendly and accommodating.

Thursday September 7
Geoff Miller, who is captaining Derbyshire in the absence of Eddie Barlow, declared just before lunch and asked me if I thought we would make a game of it. I replied that I thought we ought to . . . because it is my view that, generally speaking, no opportunity should be lost to make a finish in a Championship match.

In the evening came the end-of-season drinks party. It is traditionally thrown by the club chairman, and is generally a very convivial affair, where the committee and the players mix socially. But tonight the hospitality seemed oddly out of place. I didn't think we'd achieved much to deserve the handshakes and backslaps.

Friday September 8
The last day of term – or that is how it seems sometimes. After today, I shall play no further first-class cricket for almost two

months. It's a break that I badly need, because I found myself having to wind up the will-power to go on during the closing weeks of this season. It shouldn't get like that, and probably it wouldn't if things were more encouraging on the county front.

I was up and about early, packing clothes for the weekend ahead, and particularly for my sister's wedding in Surrey tomorrow. By ten o'clock I was at Edgbaston, chatting once again to Tiger Smith about the disappointments of the season.

As the day wore on I grew more concerned about the progress of the match. The loss of time on the first day meant inevitably that we were alternately trying to bowl them out, then to give them some runs and buy a declaration. The whole thing became totally bizarre when Alvin Kallicharran, who hasn't bowled for years, was brought on to toss up some inviting spinners – and promptly took four wickets!

We were set to score just over 250, but stage one of the innings was given over to Sacker's pursuit of his 2000th run. He scored 45 and reached his milestone, but the relative slowness of the start only put great pressure on Alvin. Ultimately, it made no difference at all. Derbyshire had played their part in trying to keep it all open, but with the match poised for a reasonable finish, the umpires offered Chris Clifford the option of coming off for bad light. Flight felt that there was no alternative – a captain's dilemma, this – and signalled the batsmen to come off. The game finished in disappointing stalemate.

It was an unsatisfactory way of bringing the season to standstill, and it left me with the feeling that we haven't really made as much progress as we might have done at Warwickshire this year. The development of David Smith and Andy Lloyd into established and promising members of the side is one of the few exceptions.

I slipped away and laid the 1978 season to rest . . . a season in which the sparkle and success of playing for England had at least been partially offset by the problems at county level from which there is never any mental escape. I was reminded to a degree of John Snow, my predecessor as England's strike bowler. At times, he found himself disillusioned by county cricket; I just hope it never happens to me.

I have never felt so tired. I am, in fact, completely drained, but I know that if I stop and do nothing I will simply go flat. With Australia so close, I can't allow that. I must think positively.

Packed in my suitcase, beneath my wedding suit, lies my tracksuit. On Sunday morning, somewhere along the country lanes of Surrey, England's new-ball bowler will be forcing himself through another five-mile run.

13
End of Term

On Monday September 11, John Whitehouse pressed an imaginary button and switched from life one to life two. Just like changing the channels of a television set. Having spent the weekend with his wife and two children, Warwickshire's cricket captain would have donned his winter 'kit' of suit, collar and tie and once again become a chartered accountant in his Nuneaton office.

On that same day, similar Cinderella-style transitions were taking place all over England. The county cricketer's ball ends, not at midnight but on that second Friday in September, and when it is past he may not become a pumpkin but he very probably turns into a fairly anonymous being, passing the winter as well as he can in a reluctant sort of hibernation.

Things are not as bad as they were. Time was when the dole queues were hideously swelled by cricketers quite unable to persuade prospective employers that they could be as much use to them for seven months of a year as any other person would be for twelve. It was nobody's fault. Just a breakdown in the system, which inevitably left a high proportion of cricketers unemployed between September and April. Those who were not among the fortunate few selected for overseas tours faced a Hobson's choice of accepting the Social Security handout, albeit with embarrassment, or filling in the time with some menial job or other. The exceptions were those, like Flight, who had been shrewd and capable enough to qualify for a career before committing themselves fully to cricket. In most cases, they always had a job and an understanding boss to go back to.

It was in the early Seventies that the county player's lot began to improve with the introduction of overseas coaching posts. They came slowly at first, mainly in the schools and clubs of South Africa. But in recent years they have spread to Australia and New Zealand. Their advantage is that they give jobs to the average county player, and his benefit is not only in terms of a secure winter but in the fact that such a job gives him ideal close-season practice. So these days the final county game of the season is also the starting pistol for many players to pack trunks, grab airline tickets and fly off in pursuit of the sun . . . and more cricket.

Warwickshire has its share of winter coaches. This year, Geoff Humpage was bound for Perth – an irony, in that he could also have been heading for Australia as England's deputy keeper if his natural talent had been more fully exploited – Andy Lloyd was flying to South Africa, Steve Rouse was taking up his regular close-season job in Rhodesia, and later on, Smithy, Art and Jasper would join the Derrick Robins Eleven in South America.

Alvin Kallicharran was looking forward to a long and rare break with his wife and son before heading for India and a six-Test series as captain of the West Indies.

David 'Barnsley' Brown went back to life on the farm, or, to be more precise, on his horse stud twenty-five miles outside Birmingham, where thirty stable boxes are gradually being filled with valuable horseflesh. Barnsley's passion for horses matches his love of cricket; he is lucky to combine the two.

Neal Abberley will split his winter three ways. He has his benefit to organize for 1979, he has a job in a travel agent's business to look after, and he will do his usual coaching stints in the Edgbaston indoor school. There he will meet up again with Steve Perryman, a home-loving man who has virtually a full-time position as indoor school coach.

That's most of the regular players, but what about Amiss and Willis?

My own plans were straightforward. Time was devoted to the commercial and promotional engagements that were necessarily neglected in such a hectic summer. I was to keep fit by running several times a week – and I was to take the rare opportunity to relax with friends and family.

Sacker's existence was not so clearly mapped out. His World Series Cricket commitments resumed in October but he would be concerned as to his cricketing future thereafter. Admirably refusing to be intimidated by the angry noises coming from the Amiss support among the members, Warwickshire's committee insisted that his dismissal stood. A special general meeting had been scheduled for September 26, but a fortnight beforehand it was cancelled. Reasons were not very clear, but it seems the group who had called it began to realize that their chances of winning a reprieve for Dennis were not high. As a compromise, it was accepted that if, during the winter months, a coexistence agreement was made between Packer and the establishment, Amiss would be welcomed back to Edgbaston for the 1979 season. It may be unlikely, but I sincerely hope that it happens, so that the differences of this summer can be fully resolved.

England's players, meanwhile, were enjoying time with their families before the gruelling four-month tour began on October 24. Most of them, even Guy the Gorilla, retreated from the headlines for a while . . . but not Geoff Boycott.

First, of course, came the expected controversy over whether he should have been elected vice-captain for the tour instead of me. Most of the newspapers, I'm told, carried letters on the subject, the majority from angry Boycott fans. Press comment inferred that it was partly through this issue that John Murray resigned as an England selector, shortly after the tour team was announced. It was three weeks before his decision was made public by a newspaper story whose timing was cruelly ironic for Geoff Boycott. For, on that very same night, Yorkshire's committee met and sacked him as captain.

Only hours earlier, Geoff had lost his mother, with whom he had always lived. It was the sort of week that even his fiercest enemies could not wish on him, and it raised doubts about whether he would even carry on playing the game he loved.

As I heard Fiery's devastating news, and felt for him, I thought too of Mike Brearley, that other central character in the summer of '78. I continued to see a fair bit of Mike during September. We share the same agent, and I also attended some of his benefit functions. In many ways Scagg is a lucky man, and I think he appreciates this. Cricket may not hold him for too many years; his interests and ambitions will lead him outside sport. But he knows he still has things to prove, paramount among them being his worth as an international-class batsman.

Australia will answer that question, perhaps, just as it will answer many more about the team being acclaimed, perhaps prematurely, as England's best in years.

By the time this is read, Australia too will be in the past. Another short break will have followed the tour, then the rituals will have begun all over again. I'll have smelt again that slightly polished mustiness about pavilions in April. Everyone at Edgbaston will have returned refreshed and enthusiastic. And I'll have been filled again with the optimism that each new season brings with it.